W9-BGN-386

FACING AD/HD

A Survival Guide for Parents of Children with Attention-Deficit/ Hyperactivity Disorder

Janet Morris

Research Press
2612 North Mattis Avenue
Champaign, Illinois 61822

Copyright © 1998 by Janet Morris

5 4 3 2 1   98 99 00 01 02

All rights reserved. Printed in the United States of America.

Excerpts may be printed in connection with published reviews in periodicals without express permission. No other part of this book may be reproduced by any means without the written permission of the publisher.

Copies of this book may be ordered from the publisher at the address given on the title page.

Cover design by Kimberly Michael
Composition by Suzanne Wagner
Printed by McNaughton & Gunn

ISBN 0-87822-381-9

Library of Congress Catalog Number 98-66602

Contents

Acknowledgments

This book and the FACES program, from which this book derives, would not have been possible without the love and support of a great many people. Ashley and Alex, you are both truly a blessing. Thank you for the multitude of gifts you give me every day. I'd also like to thank my mom and dad for their unending stamina: I'm eternally grateful for all of the lessons you have allowed me to learn in my life. Knowing that I can always count on you both to be there for me, without question, at the drop of a hat is a greater help than you'll ever know.

I'd also like to thank Barb Hosler, who showed me that dreams can come true. I don't think I'll ever know anyone else with as great a capacity as yours to encourage and support the people in this world. You are a true believer, and you give new meaning to the expression "taking the ball and running with it."

One of the things I teach in the FACES course is the necessity of having a good support network and the importance of creating that. To my network—Nancy, Becky, Kelly, Karen, Vicki, Paula, and all of those other "B" Club members and TLCer's: I thank you from the bottom of my heart. I only hope that I can be as supportive of you as you have all been for me.

Thank you also to Kath Kvols, who gave me the gift of hope. Before we even met face to face, you were an inspiration. I hope that someday I can say that I have been able to touch as many lives as you have been able to. A peaceful world truly does begin with a peaceful family.

Finally, I'd like to acknowledge Dr. John Taylor and his staff for their support of the FACES project. I appreciate your insights, guidance, and recommendations. Your dedication to the field of AD/HD is admirable.

Introduction

$\mathcal{T}$his book for parents evolved from the Families of AD/HD Children Empowerment Series (FACES), a six-session parenting course I designed and taught specifically for the parents and professionals who live and/or work with children who have AD/HD. The term *AD/HD,* which stands for Attention-Deficit/Hyperactivity Disorder, refers to all children diagnosed with this disorder, whether they are hyperactive, impulsive, and/or inattentive. I have found that the information, tools, and techniques discussed in this text are beneficial and helpful to all parent-child relationships, regardless of whether or not the child is diagnosed with AD/HD. In the FACES course I stress that there are no right or wrong ways to parent—rather only effective or ineffective parenting styles. The reason I stress this is to drop the negative, counterproductive judgments that we put on ourselves and allow others to put on us as parents. Rather than saying, "I handled that situation badly or the wrong way," it's better to say, "I handled that ineffectively. How can I be more effective next time?" The same goes with this text. It's not about teaching the one and only right way to parent, but rather effective ways to parent.

The purpose of this text is not to offer a cure-all for AD/HD. My main objective is to show that there are adjustments that can be made in your life and the lives of your children to create a more livable and peaceful situation for all involved. It can be a win-win situation if you choose it to be.

What it's all about is changing our approach to parenting. I've taken various parenting and child development courses and left them all saying, "Why isn't this working for me? For us?" The courses provided a great foundation. What I realized, though, was that I have a special situation. Children with AD/HD are special.

They are different. The approach to parenting these children must be precise and exacting. Once we realize that we aren't bad guys, nor are our children, and are willing to be open-minded about doing things differently, we can get on with improving both the quality of our lives and the lives of our children.

This book is about redirecting behaviors—our children's *and* our own. When you change your focus and your approach, it will make a noticeable difference in your behaviors and your child's. Everything in a child's environment affects his behavior, especially his parents. The goal is to create an environment that is livable and peaceful.

This book is also a culmination of seven years of research and field experience. I am a former teacher and the mother of two children diagnosed with this disorder; I grew up with family members who have it, and today some of the adults in my life also have AD/HD. I have learned that parents and professionals can minimize and even eliminate the day-in and day-out struggles and frustrations associated with AD/HD. Life doesn't have to be frustrating.

The process of change starts with taking things one day at a time. In the beginning of working toward becoming a more effective parent, it may even mean taking things one hour at a time. The situation becomes much more manageable and acceptable if you look at it and tell yourself, "I only need to think about this for the next hour." And after that hour is up, recommit for another hour, or not. If you need to take a break, do it. And then when you're up to it, recommit again.

Please don't think for a moment that because I've written a book on parenting I have achieved parental enlightenment and now am a perfect parent with perfect children. Anyone who says that is a liar. Every day, I have to recommit, to myself and to my children. Let me rephrase that: I *choose* to recommit. Every day has ups and downs. No matter what, though, if you're willing to look you can always find a positive amongst the negatives. As I typed the final revision for this book, I had a startling reminder of this. My son spilled pop on my laptop computer. And not just a little pop either. Let's put it this way—when I was able to move again, I picked up the computer, held it sideways, and watched the brown liquid pour profusely out of its side ports. I stared wide-eyed at the growing puddle under what was my lifeline to my professional future. I was not happy. It became one of those moments when I wanted to throw all this behavior management stuff right out the window and choose one of those incredibly ineffective and destructive alternatives. Realizing how angry I was, I stopped, looked at my children, and, with my teeth clenched, advised them to go to their rooms quickly. Aware of the serious nature of the situation, they immediately went.

When they were in their rooms, I blew. I screamed, I cried. All I could think of was my goal being taken from me. I had worked so hard and for so long. My research spanned over eight years. I had so much invested in this goal. I had left teaching to develop a program that in itself was a complete risk. I had given up my security to go out on this limb. The program I had developed became a reality, but for the program to reach more parents I knew I had to conform to the rules of the professional world. Even though I lived the experience every day, I had to go back to school and get some more letters after my name—in other words, a master's degree. That meant going to school full-time and teaching only occasionally. That meant next to no income. And now, with only a year left of school and a deadline to meet with the publisher, it was going to be taken away from me. All because of one lousy bottle of pop.

Needless to say, my mind was clouded with negatives. I also wanted the world to know how angry I was. This was actually good, though, because it made me call a friend: "Barb, I'm gonna kill 'em." My friend Barb, knowing me well enough, just let me go off. After about an hour of my blowing off steam, the existing negatives began to fade, and we both knew I needed to replace them with some positives. I had everything except the previous hour's work backed up. So the bottom line was either make up one hour's worth of work, which would take only another hour, or go with my anger and take those destructive alternatives. "Which would be more effective and beneficial in the long run, for both you and the kids?" Barb asked. "I need to get back to work," I said. "And I need to go give my kids a hug, tell them I love them, and talk about where their bodies should be while I'm working." It was a plan—an effective one, too. One that didn't cost my children their self-esteem or cost me mine. But it wouldn't have been an option if I had not allowed myself that break.

What was the positive in that situation? Without the event I wouldn't have written these last few paragraphs. And you might have been left thinking that this behavior stuff works only for professionals and not the average parent. Believe me, we are all average. I learned a few other things from the experience, too, the most important of which is that if I don't take care of myself, I can't take care of my kids.

Just know that challenging situations will always come up. There will be accidents, emergency trips to the doctor's office, anger, and tears. Things will get broken. It's only natural. It's all part of living and being a parent. These experiences are evened out by the positives—by experiencing the joys and sharing the laughter. For every negative experience with my children, I can honestly say there is at least one if not more positive experiences to counter it.

I made reference earlier to "perfect parents." Keep in mind that there is no such thing as a perfect parent—there are only parents who choose to educate themselves continually to become better parents. I believe this, and I believe that this book offers parents such an opportunity. There is no guarantee that six weeks after reading this book your life will be fixed. This is only the beginning of a lifelong process of coping and compensating. If you are consistent and persistent, changes, sometimes dramatic, will take place. No teacher or book can make your lives "all better." It's up to you, the parents, to make a conscious choice. Do you want your parenting to be a Band-Aid, or do you want your love to heal and sustain for a lifetime?

Chapter 1

In the Land of AD/HD

*O*nce upon a time, a baby girl was born. Her childhood was much like that of her four siblings. She attended parochial schools, spent time with friends, and took part in family functions. Eventually, while attending college, she met the man who would soon ask her to be his wife. They had a glorious wedding, and less than two years later they began their own family ... and they all lived happily ever after, right? Let's look at this scenario a little closer and in greater depth. In doing so, you may be able to relate to some of the details left out of the story.

I was born into a family that had a history of AD/HD, although at that time it went by one of its aliases: hyperkinesis. Two family members were officially diagnosed with it. While attending college I met and married a wonderful and also very energetic man. Soon afterwards, we did what all young couples do before they start a family: We got a puppy to practice parenting on. I've always been a firm believer that there's a reason for everything, and in the case of this puppy somebody somewhere was trying to tell me something. It turned out that the dog was hyperactive. We decided to make the dog an outside dog instead of an inside dog. That solved that problem.

Taking no heed of this prophetic sign, we started our family sixteen months later with the birth of our first child, Ashley Christine. I had an uncomfortable pregnancy with a few health problems, one of which was preeclampsia. A strange aspect of my pregnancy was the amount of fetal movement. Though she was three weeks overdue, Ashley never stopped moving. She was always in motion, poking and prodding at my insides. When labor was induced (finally!), it was very difficult. At birth Ashley didn't breathe right away; when she did catch her first breath, it was followed by a loud cry. It was the most beautiful sound in the world, or so we thought. It soon came back to haunt us. Two weeks later, that same cry began again and continued, seemingly nonstop. Ashley had developed colic, which lasted until she was six months old. And so began the midnight car rides—one of the few ways to get her to sleep. I might mention here that colic, like AD/HD, is not caused by bad parenting or a nervous mother, but rather has a biological basis. Early on in this ordeal I was lucky to stumble upon a wonderful device. Invented by a pediatrician for his own child, it came in two small pieces, attached to the crib, and simulated the sound and motion of a car ride. I used to take that sound box with me everywhere I went, with spare batteries just in case. The device made a sound like static and, though it was sometimes annoying to others, it was much more pleasant than Ashley's cry from the pain of colic. (Colic cries are different from regular cries—more intense and higher pitched.)

Soon after the onset of colic came another one of those "cute" behavioral traits we associated later with AD/HD. Ashley didn't like to sleep—at all. I would rock her for what seemed like forever, keeping my body perfectly still so as not to disturb any progress I was making in her dozing off. Her body would eventually relax and her eyelids begin to droop. I'd think, "Yes! We're almost there!" as her eyes would begin to roll back and her eyelids drooped even more. Then she would flinch. She was revitalized and ready for another round! I thought to myself, "This is not good—she's four weeks old and already knows how to keep herself awake." I don't know how I knew the reason she stayed awake was that she was curious and didn't want to miss anything. Finally, I caught on. I would drape a blanket over her head and my shoulder, as if I were nursing her, to shut out the world that was keeping her from sleep.

Admittedly, some resentment was beginning to grow, but it was quickly squelched by Ashley's personality. She seemed to go from one extreme to another. If she wasn't fussing she was very happy and playful—extremely playful. Her development continued at what I can now see was a very rapid pace. The first noticeable sign of this was early development of her gross motor skills. She walked at six months. No, that wasn't a typo—I really did mean six months. Not toddling, not creeping, but walking. This was soon followed by a lifelong phase of getting into things. We rapidly childproofed everything in sight. Much to our dismay, this didn't really work. It is not unusual for some children with AD/HD to have a knack for getting into things they're not supposed to, including childproofed cabinets. The irony of this struck me one day when I had to ask my daughter to open a locked cabinet that I wasn't able to get into. This also explains my advocacy of duct tape as the world's greatest childproofing tool. (No, it is not to be used on the child!) Whatever you don't want the child to get into, duct tape it shut. The reason is that you can hear duct tape being pulled off and can usually intervene before any serious harm occurs. But you can't hear those special locks being opened, and you may not be able to intervene in time. Duct tape does look tacky, but appearances aren't everything, and, in the case of raising a child, safety is.

Ashley's verbal skills also developed at an early age. By the age of two, she could carry on a very complete and rational conversation with anyone. People were always amazed by this. A petite child, she resembled a doll that could walk and talk. It was my first experience parenting a two-year-old, so I thought Ashley's motor and verbal development was normal. What didn't seem normal to me was her behavior. It was so extreme—she was so busy. The phrase "terrible twos" was a gross understatement in her case. Looking back, I can see all of the indicators that would later point to her diagnosis of AD/HD:

- At age one she had learned to climb out of her crib and was smart enough to throw out her pillows first to land on.

- She was impulsive, never giving a thought to possible dangers. If the door was open she would take off, heading directly for the street and traffic.

- Occasionally, her destructiveness would make itself very apparent. I remember the time she got into a childproofed cabinet (pre-duct-tape days) and proceeded to paint pictures on the wall with red nail polish. We also had to make sure that her crib was far enough away from the wall so that she could not peel the wallpaper off or pull the curtains down.

Ashley never sat and played with one thing at a time. Her play consisted of playing with everything in the room simultaneously.

By the time she turned three I was seriously doubting my ability to be a parent. I obviously couldn't handle a child; just look at the lousy job I was doing. My self-esteem was shot. The majority of my day was spent in anger and frustration. Again, Ashley's extremes were evident, with seemingly no middle ground. The more she did, the angrier I got. I couldn't control her. And then, just when I'd begin to think that one of us, either her or me, needed to be committed, she would do something wonderful, and I'd fall in love with her all over again. Then I would hate myself for hating her, and the cycle of low self-esteem would begin all over again.

I'll never forget her first day of preschool. I was the proud mom sending my daughter off on the first step of her academic career. I was so nervous, and she was so cool about it, like it was no big deal. I dropped her off and drove around trying to find something to do to occupy my time. Finally, the moment arrived to pick her up. She came running up to me, smiling, and I asked excitedly, "How was your day?" She responded with "Mommy, all they did was tell me, 'Sit down! Sit down! Sit down!'" I stepped back, feeling a jump of excitement in my stomach and thought to myself, "Yes!" Finally, someone else had noticed. It wasn't just me. This was the beginning of enlightenment for me, and I started putting the pieces of the puzzle together. We had a wonderful pediatrician who, unbeknownst to me, had also been putting the pieces together each time he had seen Ashley. By the time I said to him, "Look, I think this is what's going on," he responded with, "I think you're right, and it's time we found out for sure." He referred us to a specialist, and the diagnostic process began.

Once Ashley was diagnosed, I was relieved. I wasn't insane, nor was she. There was a logical and physical explanation for everything that was happening. So everything would be all better now, right? Now we can live happily ever after, right? Wrong. I had an explanation, but I didn't have a cure. No one did. The question now was "How do we live with this?" I began the long process of research and education.

It took quite a bit of self-talk before I could think of having another child. Ashley already took up so much of my time, though treatment had made a tremendous difference in all of our lives. Things were getting better and slightly easier, and we seemed to enjoy each other more than ever. But there was still a fear lingering in the back of my mind: "What if we have another child with AD/HD?" And then I thought, "Nah . . . it could never happen twice."

And, basically, it didn't. Our son, Alex, was born shortly before Ashley's third birthday. It was a relatively normal pregnancy, and labor and delivery were problem-free. From the start, Alex had a much different temperament than Ashley did, and I breathed a sigh of relief. But then, when he was about a month old, he also developed colic. His colic was much worse and lasted longer than his sister's had. That was the only similarity they had, though. Everything else seemed to be progressing along normally, or so I thought. Developmentally, Alex was much slower than Ashley. Though still within the normal range, he was at the far end of the developmental scale in all of his skills. He was just over a year old when he began to walk. At two he was still using telegraphic speech patterns: "Big dog!" "Fire truck!"

We began to notice Alex's temper at the age of two. Unlike Ashley, his temperament was not extreme. He was usually in that middle ground—basically pretty calm and content. But when something didn't go his way, all hell broke loose. His anger was the one emotion that was extreme. He would throw himself down on the floor, kicking and screaming. Soon these fits of anger became more and more common, and I began to feel that knot in my stomach again. I had no clue how to handle these explosive outbursts, and in the back of my mind was that nagging thought "It's happening again." After a lot of soul searching and asking myself, "Why me? Why is this happening again?" I finally realized I did not have another child just like Ashley. I had Alex. He also had AD/HD, but in a very different way than his sister. I'm a firm believer that there are reasons for everything. At the time I didn't know what the reason was for my having two children with this disorder, but I knew that someday I would know. So many times we find ourselves asking the question "Why me?" The answer is simple: "Why not me?" There must be a reason, and someday it will be apparent. For now, though, as parents we need to start asking ourselves, "What can I do about it?" That's when things will begin to change.

CHANGING YOUR MIND-SET

I learned a long time ago the importance of the mind-set in dealing with this disorder. Looking at things from a different perspective—from a different mind-set—initially can be very difficult, but it's the first step in the journey toward establishing a more stable and enjoyable way of life. It is the key to a peaceful coexistence. It means the ability to see your child as a pure and joyous spirit, as a gift given just to you and made especially for you. If in the back of your mind you are saying, "Some gift!" that's the old mind-set, the resentment, the anger, and the frustration. If that's how you choose to continue viewing this child, the journey that follows will be very bumpy. When you consciously decide to see things differently, peace can begin.

As parents we have to be able to say, "This isn't working for me or you. We need to do this differently. We need to have a new approach." As parents of children with AD/HD, it is crucial for us to be flexible and adaptable. Being flexible is knowing when the time is right to deal with a situation. In this way our children are our teachers. They show us what they want to learn and when they're able to learn it and how much they can handle at a time.

It has been said that our children are really angels who choose us specifically for a reason. In the beginning I didn't see it this way. I was overwhelmed emotionally with all the negative aspects of coping with the situation. I know now that my children have taught me compassion, patience, loving tolerance, and unconditional love. The ability to see my children in this new light gave me the desire to do things differently, the willingness to change.

In doing things differently I realized I needed to face my challenges. There is a story that makes this point very clear: On the African plains the lionesses do the hunting for the pride. Both old and young lionesses will take part in the hunt. The young ones have the speed, agility, and sharp teeth to catch the prey, but the old ones have one advantage over them—a loud, fierce roar. So when they go out to hunt, the young ones go in one direction, and the old ones go in the other, both hiding in the tall grass. The old ones begin to roar wildly and fiercely, and the prey, hearing this, are overcome by fear and run the opposite way, directly into the jaws of the young lionesses. If only they would have run toward the roar, they might have lived. The moral of the story is that you must face your fears and challenges and "run to the roar" because those challenges are really opportunities to live life more fully.

NO ONE IS JUNE CLEAVER

At this point you may be beginning to doubt and shake your head and say to yourself, "She makes this sound like an episode of *Ozzie and Harriet* or *Leave It to Beaver.* Like it's so easy and

13

simple, but it's not!" This is not *Leave It to Beaver,* nor is anyone June Cleaver, but it can be simple and easy. So many times I hear parents say, "I don't know what to do anymore. I've tried everything." I believe them because I know that this was true for me as well. But this is also the problem. We get input from all kinds of sources, all of whom have good intentions. We hear "You should try this" and "You should try that" or "You're too hard on him" or "You're too easy on him." What we have to remember is that our children are special. Our children are different, and parenting them has to be special and different also. You cannot approach these children with "regular" parenting techniques. You have to come at parenting from a whole different approach. That's what this book is all about.

WHAT IS AD/HD?

AD/HD has gone under as many as seventy-five different names in the course of its documented history, which goes back over a hundred years. Some of the more prevalent ones were minimal brain dysfunction, hyperkinesis, and behavioral disorder. In the early 1980s, the medical profession called this constellation of symptoms Attention Deficit Disorder (ADD) and Attention Deficit Hyperactivity Disorder (ADHD). In 1994, the fourth edition of the *Diagnostic and Statistical Manual of Mental Disorders* (DSM-IV), basically the Webster's dictionary for the field of mental health, gave us the latest term: Attention-Deficit/Hyperactivity Disorder, or AD/HD.

When an earlier edition of the DSM, as it is known, first came out with the term ADD back in the 1980s it was wonderful because we finally had a comprehensive name for the disorder. However, the term did not encompass all of the various forms of the disorder. People used other terms, like ADDH, ADHD, ADD hyperactive, ADD hypoactive, and ADD undifferentiated, among others.

The evidence suggests AD/HD is not one specific disorder with different variations, but really three subtypes: AD/HD predominantly inattentive type, AD/HD predominantly hyperactive-impulsive type, and AD/HD combined type. These subtypes take in all the various aspects and forms of AD/HD. For example, some children with the disorder may have little or no trouble sitting still or inhibiting behavior but may have great difficulty attending and focusing on a task. Others may be able to stay on task and focus but have great difficulty controlling their behavior—in other words, they are impulsive and/or hyperactive and thus lose their focus once involved in a task. (See the appendix for complete DSM-IV diagnostic criteria.)

It's helpful to think of a scale with the symptomatic behaviors of the disorder falling into different areas. The right end of the scale is severe, and the left end is mild, with moderate falling in the center. A child could be severely inattentive (toward the extreme right of the scale) but only mildly to moderately hyperactive/impulsive (toward the left end of the scale)—or vice versa. In other words, the child's symptomatic behaviors could fall on different areas of the scale.

Mild	Moderate	Severe

Symptomatic behaviors
(inattentiveness, impulsivity, hyperactivity)

Chapter 1

This is why two children with the diagnosis of AD/HD can display their symptomatic behaviors in very different ways. My own two children are both diagnosed as having AD/HD with coexisting oppositional defiant disorder. Though they share the same diagnosis, they display their symptomatic behaviors in very different ways. Ashley is severely hyperactive but only mildly defiant. Alex, on the other hand, is only mildly hyperactive but severely defiant. Thus my reasoning that though it may have happened to me twice, it happened in very different ways.

One of the reasons I am going into so much detail on AD/HD terminology is that I want no one to feel slighted. This book covers all aspects of living or working with a child affected by any of the three subtypes: predominantly hyperactive-implusive, predominantly inattentive, or combined. Think of it like this: Say you are going grocery shopping for some soup. You know you want soup but what kind—chicken noodle, cream of potato, or beef vegetable? They're all soups, just different kinds. It's the same with AD/HD. The three subcomponents are different kinds of the disorder. Just as soup is a broad, generic name, AD/HD is a broad, generic name. For the rest of this book the disorder will be referred to as AD/HD.

We know what to call it, but what is it? AD/HD is a chemical imbalance in the frontal lobe of the brain at the neurotransmitter site responsible for attending to and focusing on tasks. At this one small spot in this person's body, there is actually less activity going on than normal, kind of like an electrical short. There is also some new evidence of a lower rate of the brain's use of glucose. Estimates vary, but according to Dr. Russell Barkley, this neurobiologically based developmental disability is thought to affect 3 to 5 percent of the school-age population.

AD/HD is a genetic disorder; it is inherited and passed on from generation to generation. When parents first hear this, one sometimes responds with "Well, it didn't come from MY family," then the other responds with "It certainly didn't come from MY family." I've got news for you—if you look at your family trees you may not find anyone diagnosed with this disorder, but you will probably find people like Uncle Joe, the workaholic, or Aunt Betty, whose house was always compulsively spotless, or Cousin Billy, who went from job to job to job, or Cousin Sally, who went from husband to husband to husband. There may have been someone who was an alcoholic, a drifter, an overachiever, or an underachiever. What's important is not where the disorder came from but what we can do with it.

So, the disorder is genetic and biological—there is a chemical imbalance in the brain. Environmental factors can have an effect on the extent to which the disorder makes itself known, but they are not the cause. AD/HD is not caused by bad parenting or being a nervous parent, nor is it caused by a teacher the child had or by that time you left him with a sitter or by your watching that scary movie when you were six months pregnant. In the classroom I explain it in the following manner: Say a child is born with the genetic coding for diabetes. If she eats only a healthful diet through adulthood, she will more than likely not show any diabetic tendencies until her diet changes and she starts eating less healthful foods. But if that same child is born with the same tendency from birth and is given nothing but sugary and unhealthful foods, she will more than likely demonstrate diabetic tendencies at an earlier age. It's the same with AD/HD: If a child is born into a family that is highly structured and/or more tolerant of a range of behaviors, she may not show any problems until she enters school. This is not to say that school is the cause of the problem behavior, but rather that school is a new and different environment. This also explains and dispels another myth. Did you ever hear your child's caretaker say, "She doesn't act that way with me"? Kids with AD/HD do interact differently in different environments.

The fact that AD/HD is a genetic, biological disorder is a difficult concept for some people to understand. This is because, other than these children's activity level, there is no tangible sign. They aren't on crutches, nor are telethons organized to raise money for research. Outwardly, they appear "normal," but inside there is chaos. It's easy for us to feel sympathy and compassion for the parents of an obviously physically challenged child, but many times we are quick to judge the parents of children who have AD/HD. Not one of us can honestly say, when seeing a child misbehave in public, that our first reaction has never been "Can't those parents control that child?" Acceptance of the reality of this disorder and of this child's special needs may come easier if we as a society take responsibility for our part and become less quick to judge others. What if the next time we see a child misbehaving in public we think, "I bet those parents feel really challenged and could use some support"?

There's a theory that if parents use the right techniques and have a good relationship with their child, then the child will grow up happy and well-adjusted. If he doesn't, then it's the parents' fault. Part of this theory is true; however, you cannot apply standard childrearing techniques and methods to a child with AD/HD and expect them to work. Another theory is that the child's behavior is a predictable reaction to negative and overcontrolling parental behavior. This theory is puzzling because it assumes that the influence is only in one direction—from parent to child—and that child behavior has no effect on parent reactions. Infants are born with different temperamental styles, obvious from the first moments of life. Some are easygoing; others are more vigorous and intense. The behavior of an intense or difficult infant can push even the most patient parents over the edge. These parents quickly learn to treat this child differently because his behavior demands a different approach. Just as some of the child's behavior is a response to parental behavior, parental behavior is also a response to the child's behavior. On a positive note, these patterns are not etched in stone; changes in the child can bring about changes in the parent, and, more importantly, changes in the parent can bring about changes in the child. Although childrearing practices and environment have some effect on the child's behavior, they are not the cause of AD/HD.

JUST A FAD?

Lately, it seems just about anyone you talk to knows someone affected with AD/HD. When teaching, I usually at some point am asked the questions "Why are we hearing so much about this now?" and "Isn't this just a fad?" AD/HD is no more a fad than diabetes, epilepsy, or depression. It has always been here, just under different names. And often these names were not as socially acceptable as AD/HD. The first official mention of the disorder in medical journals was about a hundred years ago. Researchers have traced it back much further than this by studying the documented medical and behavioral histories of various people. Did you know that Eleanor Roosevelt, Albert Einstein, and Abraham Lincoln may have had AD/HD? It has even been theorized that AD/HD has been around since the beginning of humankind. The greatest numbers of people with AD/HD can be found in the United States and Australia. Let's think about why this might be: The first white settlers on our shores were people who were unhappy with life where they were, made trouble by speaking their minds, were restless and frustrated, and got up and left. They were adventurous explorers, not wanting to stay in one place and always looking for new horizons. They were considered a rebellious lot, eventually even starting a revolution and defiantly demanding their rights. And then there's Australia, originally a penal colony for Britain. Its first inhabitants from the "civilized" world were convicts, people who do things without realizing the consequences of their actions. These may be coincidences, but I don't think so.

We are fortunate to live in a society today that is more aware and accepting of AD/HD than in the past. Our diagnostic procedures have become much more accurate—they now allow for the diagnosis of coexisting disorders. In the 1970s a child who showed symptomatic behaviors of a conduct disorder and AD/HD would have been diagnosed simply with conduct disorder. Now we can acknowledge any coexisting disorders in the diagnosis and address each appropriately.

Earlier, I mentioned environmental influences. Along this line is another reason we hear more about AD/HD now than thirty or forty years ago. Our society has undergone many changes since then, including the various roles within the family. In the 1950s and 1960s, when the Nelsons and the Cleavers were popular family role models, the majority of family households had two parents and a single income. And the neighborhoods were safe to play in. Kids came home from school and hurried to get their homework done because then they could go out and play— running and jumping until the streetlights came on. Then they would come home and go to bed, physically drained from all that exercise. Nowadays we don't have the luxury of those same family roles: Many family households are single parent/single income, or two parent/two income. After-school care has become a necessity for many families, including my own. Children who used to exert themselves for hours after school running around the neighbor- hood now go directly from one environment (school) that confines them to their seats to another (day care) that also confines them to a limited area. The point is not that these societal changes are wrong, but that because of them the symptomatic behavior of AD/HD is more likely to cause problems.

Another reason we hear so much about AD/HD today is that there have been many negative reports in the media about the abuse of medication used to treat the disorder—specifically, reports of teens "snorting" methylphenidate (Ritalin), the drug most com- monly used to treat AD/HD. I find it interesting that the media focuses on Ritalin but that we rarely hear reports of other abuse, such as kids snorting aspirin, blood pressure or depression med- ications, or even powdered detergents and cleaners. In the case of Ritalin abuse, the problem is not the particular medication but the child's need to abuse it. This abuse is due to a lack of knowledge and is evidence of the need to accurately and continually educate ourselves about AD/HD and its treatment.

I'd like to dispel another common myth about AD/HD. The disorder is not outgrown. It does not go away, but it may change forms as the child gets older, especially during puberty. A severely hyperactive child may become less "hyper" as a teen but may become more easily distracted or prone to making impulsive or rash decisions—or the situation could be reversed. The symptomatic behaviors may change and become weaker or stronger, but the underlying disorder is always there.

A THOROUGH DIAGNOSIS

Your and your child's journey with AD/HD is a lifelong process. And though I cannot provide you with all of the answers—no one can—this text can give you the basic tools to compensate, cope, and maintain your sanity on this adventure. But before you can take the first step in working with this disorder, your child must undergo a very thorough diagnostic procedure. I'll have more to say about diagnosis in chapter 5.

There is no blood test for AD/HD—testing for it is a process of elimination. We have to rule out any and all imitator disorders, and there are a multitude of them: anxiety disorders, depression, learning disorders (such as central auditory processing disorders), hearing and vision problems, and even food allergies, to name a few. A comprehensive assessment of your child should begin with a complete physical exam, including blood work to test for any allergies.

There is a difference between a food allergy and AD/HD. A child with a food allergy will display symptomatic behaviors similar to those of AD/HD, but if you remove the offending food from that child's diet, the behavior will dissipate. If a child has AD/HD, it doesn't matter what you remove from her diet—the behavior will persist. This is not an excuse, though, to let your child eat whatever she wants. Any child should have a healthy, well-balanced diet. But realize when someone says to you, "You just let that child eat too much sugar and food with dyes. That's why she's hyper," that is not true for a child who has AD/HD.

After the physical examination, the diagnostic process should continue with academic assessments; tests for intelligence, social and emotional functioning, and developmental abilities; and measures of attention span and impulsivity. It's interesting to note that for the most part, kids with AD/HD usually have a slightly higher IQ than those without the disorder. So the problem is not a matter of "being smart"—it lies in the area of attention, not intelligence.

At some point in the testing procedure the diagnostician will ask for medical histories and behavioral backgrounds for you and your spouse, as well as for your child. This is part of the process of elimination. The diagnostician will more than likely go over a list of AD/HD indicators with you, like the one that follows. Normally, when I read this list in a workshop, I ask parents to take part by raising their hands when they hear an indicator that they can relate to in their own children. If they can relate a little bit I ask them to wave their raised hand a little bit, and if they can relate a lot, to wave their hand a lot. The first time I took part in this kind of activity I was in the back of the audience with both hands raised (two kids, remember), waving wildly!

Please remember that these are only *possible* indicators. But if they are all present in some form, more than likely we're dealing with AD/HD. Interestingly, many of these indicators can be found in the average person. It's part of being human, or having "humanitis," as some people call it. We all have times when we're forgetful, or have sudden bursts of energy, or become impatient. For someone with AD/HD, however, these indicators are the rule and not the exception. I mentioned earlier that diagnosing this disorder is a process of elimination. That process is also like putting together a puzzle: Think of these indicators as puzzle pieces. If all of the pieces are there and fit together, then we have a clear picture of AD/HD. If we have only a couple of pieces, then we don't have a finished picture.

INDICATORS OF AD/HD

Notably higher level of prebirth activity

Health problems in pregnancy (preeclampsia, eclampsia, high blood pressure, alcohol and/or drug abuse, smoking)

First pregnancy

Long labor

Birth injury or lack of oxygen

Birth defects

Prematurity or postmaturity

Irregular sleep patterns

Intense temperament

Colic

Frequent colds or upper respiratory infections

Poor bonding

Low tolerance for change

Unusual crib behavior (climbing out, excessive rocking)

Rapid or delayed development of motor and language skills

Sleep problems

Hyperactivity

Impulsivity

Unawareness of natural consequences

Destructive behavior

Aggressive behavior

INDICATORS OF AD/HD CONTINUED

Gastrointestinal problems

Poor coordination

Negative confrontational behavior

Family history of AD/HD

Inattention to detail or tendency to make careless mistakes in tasks

Difficulty sustaining attention in tasks or activities

Failure to follow instructions or to finish tasks

Difficulty organizing tasks

Avoidance or dislike of tasks that require sustained attention (homework, chores)

Distractibility

Forgetfulness in daily activity

Fidgeting with hands or feet or squirming in seat

Leaving seat in situations in which being seated is expected

Running or climbing at inappropriate times (in adults may be limited to feelings of restlessness)

Difficulty playing or engaging in leisure activities quietly

Being "on the go" or acting as if "driven by a motor"

Excessive talking

Answering before a question is completed

Difficulty awaiting turn

Tendency to interrupt or intrude on others

WHAT AD/HD FEELS LIKE

What does it feel like to have AD/HD? A close friend gave me a wonderful description. "You know when you go into a department store and you're in the electronics department? In front of you are fifty television screens, all with different stations on. The volume is turned up on all of them, and you're trying to watch everything at once. You hear babies crying, people laughing, music playing, bells ringing. It's really annoying!" When I heard this, I thought, "How true." Her description explains the filter problem. AD/HD people are filterless! Sound strange? Let me explain.

Like computers, human beings obtain knowledge through the intake of information. But where computers might take in data through a keyboard, we use our five senses: sight, smell, taste, touch, and hearing. Every bit of information we've ever obtained has had to come through one of these senses. Information enters through one or more of the senses, then goes through a "filtering system" in the brain's frontal lobe, from which it is sent to the area of the brain that can utilize it. People who are not affected by AD/HD can filter the information as it comes through—that is, they can focus on the intake of information that is pertinent at the time and block out the other information coming in from the other senses. People with AD/HD cannot do this; their filtering systems are not up to par. They take in all their information simultaneously.

Therefore, when we say to a child, "Why aren't you paying attention to me?" we need to remember that a hundred other stimuli are competing for his attention. We wouldn't think of asking a diabetic not to be affected by sugar, yet we ask and sometimes even demand that this child pay attention, something he's not capable of doing on his own.

Regarding the senses, let me explain one other thing. It's common for people with AD/HD to be hypersensitive. In other words, their five senses are stronger than other people's. For example, these are the kids who want the tags cut out of their clothing because they can't stand the rubbing on their skin. Or you may have heard that giving a young child a warm bath before bed will relax her. This is true for most people, but not necessarily for those with AD/HD. The feeling of the water on their skin may actually wind them up. It's the same with back rubs. Another example pertains to the sense of smell: My daughter can smell broccoli cooking in the kitchen when she's outside, a hundred feet away in the backyard. And this heightened awareness is true for all of their senses; what goes unnoticed by us can be extremely distracting to them. Remember, too, they take in all their information simultaneously. Everything that's going on in the world around them affects them all at once.

But if this is true, why can kids with AD/HD focus so well on a TV or a computer? Think about it. Television has taken all the distractions of the outside world and incorporated them onto a small screen. It's so distracting that it becomes attracting. It's the same with computers: The feel of the computer keys, the humming of the CPU unit, the sound effects of the programs, and the images on the screen all require a child to use several senses simultaneously. Again, it's so distracting that it's attracting. So, this aspect of AD/HD—hypersensitivity—needs to be understood clearly in order for you to work effectively with your child.

A CHILD'S VIEWPOINT

Something that can help you change your mind-set and that will give you a new and different perspective on AD/HD is to see the world through your child's eyes. Believe it or not, he doesn't want to act the way he does. He literally cannot help or contain himself. Did you ever have a situation when you looked at your child and asked, "Why did you do that?" only to get a blank stare in return? It's because he truly doesn't know why. He's clueless. I remember one day while my daughter was still very young, about two. I walked into the kitchen and found her on top of the refrig-erator. "Ashley, what are you doing?" I asked. She responded with that familiar blank stare. I then said, "Where is your body right now?" She looked around: "On top of the frigelator" (that's what she used to call it). I responded, "Um-hmm, and where should your body be?" "Down there," she said, pointing to the floor. I helped her down. Why was she up there? Because that's where I used to keep the junk food. The point is that most of the time, kids with AD/HD don't recognize their behavior unless it is clearly defined and pointed out to them. All that registers for them is that "Oh no, I'm getting yelled at again" feeling.

Several years ago a study was done at Michigan State University by Dr. Maria Rohrkemper, and reported by Dr. Barbara Ingersoll. Rohrkemper asked a random sample of junior high school students to view a video of a working classroom—that is, a normal group of students working and interacting in a classroom. The sample group was to observe how the teacher interacted with the students. The video included some interactions between teacher and students that demonstrated encouragement and some that demonstrated stu-dents being redirected or reprimanded. The sample group was then asked to give feedback on the actions of the teacher. When it came to her actions with a student who was redirected or reprimanded, some of the group agreed that what she did was the best course of action while others disagreed, saying that she was way out of line and had no right to pick on the kid. The sample group was then tested for cognitive skills and abilities or disabilities. The children who agreed that the teacher had taken the correct course of action with her student all tested "normal," while the children who said she was out of line all tested positive for AD/HD. From this we can conclude that, for the most part, kids with AD/HD don't recognize their behavior or its effects on others. Instead, they feel that the world is against them.

When such kids do recognize their behaviors, they are usually the behaviors that have repeatedly gotten them into trouble. The kids know criticism will soon follow because that's the established pattern. As parents and educators, we have a habit of telling a child only what she's doing wrong, thinking this will prevent future misbehavior. Then we wonder why the child has low self-esteem, is frustrated, or feels like a failure. Even statements like "You can do better than that" aren't serving the child. What then goes through her mind is "Why bother? I'll just mess it up again." We have to replace the negative with the positive. We all have periods of low self-esteem, but for a child with AD/HD it's a constant underlying factor. Her self-esteem is like a bright light that has been covered with many layers of paint. The light is her true self, and the layers of paint are how the world responds to her. It should be our goal as parents to stop any more layers from being added and to chip away at the old layers until the bright light shines through.

REALIZING CHOICE IN BEHAVIOR

I am in no way making excuses for the behavior of children with AD/HD. I am saying that they don't realize they have choices in their behavior. It is our responsibility to teach them that they can choose to act ineffectively or effectively and that they will be held accountable for their actions, whether they are good, bad, effective, or ineffective. Having AD/HD does not excuse someone from being responsible for his behavior; it just explains why the behavior is going on. I remember a case where a person had committed a very serious crime, and his defense was that he did it because he had AD/HD. Although that explains why he acted on impulse, he still had to be held accountable for his behavior, which, thank goodness, he was. Once we have clearly defined the child's behavior, his responsibility in that behavior, and the consequences of his choices of behavior, we can then hold him accountable.

Chapter 2

Basic Tools for Teaching and Learning

*P*arenting a child with AD/HD always begins with the same first step. It's the secret ingredient in the recipe for becoming a more effective parent. The first step in parenting these children is . . . to do absolutely nothing. Sound crazy? It's not. Technically, it's called observation, and it is critically important in changing behaviors. If you sit back and watch your child, she will teach you what you need to be teaching her. I'm not saying that you should sit still and watch while the house falls down around you. What I am saying is watch your child and, as much as possible, keep doing whatever it is that you normally do. If you need to intervene, do so, but don't get all wound up about it. Instead, observe and take notes.

Start an observation journal in which you keep track of whatever is going on in the environment when an undesirable behavior occurs. Write it all down: what your child was wearing, what activity he had just come from, what your part in the behavior was, whether you asked him to do something, the time of day, whether the TV was on—whatever was going on at the time. After a week or two you will start to see patterns develop. And from those patterns you will be able to note triggers for the behaviors. From those identified patterns, pick the behavior that bugs you the most—this is your target behavior. You will focus your energies on this, and only this, behavior. In this way you can be persistent and consistent.

PERSISTENCY WITH CONSISTENCY

As I mentioned in chapter 1, parenting a child with AD/HD requires a whole different approach. That approach depends on several things, including observation and the idea of being persistent and consistent. Do you know the expression "I did it until I was blue in the face"? Well, with this child you won't do it 'till you're blue in the face, but 'till you're past blue and turning purple and think you're going to pass out from lack of oxygen—and then you'll keep on going because you're on the verge of a breakthrough. There is a trick to this, though: You only try to change one behavior at a time. It is impossible to be consistent and persistent with all of this child's behaviors simultaneously. You'll become frustrated and eventually you'll give up. Only handle one thing at a time. I'm not saying to ignore the other behaviors. Just don't focus all of your energy on them. It's natural for us as parents to want to fix these problems all at once and be rid of them. But it doesn't work that way—not with a child with AD/HD or even with a "normal" child. There will always be new problems to face. Do not expect that you can handle everything to perfection. Such expectations are nothing more than premeditated resentments, and perfectionism is a form of insanity. Eliminate them both right now.

Being persistent and consistent is also about prioritizing and not sweating the small stuff. In other words, handle what's most important and pertinent at the time, and don't worry about the other issues. They will get handled in time.

One of the first target behaviors I worked on with my son was going to bed. I'm sure you can relate to the idea that we can handle just about anything that goes on in a day as long as the kids go to bed at night so we can get a little break. Alex was about three when I started working with him on this target behavior. After observing the situation, I wrote down some ideas for a bedtime routine for Alex. I then sat down with him and explained my ideas (remember, he was only three at the time). It went something like this: "Alex,

you know how you don't like to go to bed at night and I sometimes get mad at you about that, and then you get mad at me? I
have an idea so we don't get mad anymore. And we get to put this
idea on a big board, and you get to color it. Doesn't that sound
cool?" So we set out to make his bedtime chart. I got some posterboard and on it I wrote the words, and he drew pictures about the
words and colored them. A similar chart (without the drawings of
a three-year-old) follows.

ALEX'S BEDTIME CHART

7:00   Bath time! (Remember to pick up
before you wash up.)

7:30   PJ's (Would you like a snack after
your pj's are on?)

7:35   Quiet time

8:15   Brush teeth

8:20   Tuck-in (Which two songs will you
choose tonight?)

8:30   Lights out (Sweet dreams!)

When we finished the chart I asked Alex when he wanted to
start his new, cool bedtime routine—in two nights from now or
three? He said, "Two!" And I said, "Great!" For the next two days
we talked on and off about our cool bedtime routine. We also
talked about what would happen if he chose to get out of bed after
8:30. I would remind him (calmly) of where he should be and
walk him back to bed, and there would be no more talking. When

the night came I was ready to follow through with my commitment. We followed the chart perfectly. "What do you get to do now?" I asked. "I get to get my jammies on!" Alex responded. "Great! Go ahead and do that," I said. We did this with each point on the chart, all the way through to bedtime.

After I tucked him in I walked out of his room and started downstairs. Halfway down I heard his familiar scampering. Without a word, I turned, put my hand on his shoulder lightly, and walked him back to bed. No hug or kiss or interaction. I headed back downstairs. Guess what? Same thing happened. So I did my part again and stated calmly, "You need to be in bed now," and walked back out. Again I started down the stairs, and you know what happened? You guessed it! There he was, right behind me. This little pattern of ours continued on thirty-seven times. Yes, thirty-seven. I had made a commitment, though, and I remained calmly persistent in that commitment. And I was consistent with my actions. That night it took thirty-seven tries before Alex finally stayed in bed, but you know what? The next night it took us only thirty-four times, and the night after that, thirty-three. This continued until it was down to only one time.

Why would I want to put myself through this? Why not just yell at him or spank him? Because those things won't change his behavior. The routine and pattern that we created did. And that's the goal, to create effective, healthy, lifelong behaviors. And that's also why you target only one behavior at a time. If I attempted to change all of Alex's problem behaviors at once, and tried to be this consistent and persistent with all of them simultaneously, I'd be nuts after two days! Then I'd go back to spanking and yelling and shaming, only to leave myself feeling guilty and inadequate and my child feeling frustrated—not to mention that I wouldn't have changed those problem behaviors. So focus your energies on one target behavior at a time, work with it until you're successful, and then go on to another target. This doesn't mean that you've eliminated that problem behavior completely. You'll still need to reinforce your work on occasion, but the behavior will definitely not need the focus or energy that it once did.

In the last example we saw not only what persistency with consistency can accomplish, we also saw the advantages of a routine. Implementing routines and structure is of great benefit to children with AD/HD and their families. But that doesn't mean you should turn your home into a command center with a schedule similar to that of an international airline. As with all aspects of behavior management, you have to take it slow and do only one thing at a time. This includes routines and structure, which will be discussed further in chapter 4.

MANAGING TRANSITIONS

As you observe your child, you will probably notice that a prime time for misbehavior or difficulties is when she is involved in some sort of transition. Transitions wreak havoc with children who have AD/HD. They do much better in an environment that provides a foundation of routines and structure. Transitions are any time you change from one thing to another, whether you are starting an activity, doing something out of the ordinary, or even facing a change in the environment. The example I gave earlier of Alex's bedtime difficulties involved a transition, moving from one activity to another. Because transitions are difficult for children with AD/HD, the more you can implement routines at a gradual pace, the better. Again, it's crucial to go slowly and build up to transitions, especially when it involves something out of the norm. Many of you probably dread holidays. I used to, but not anymore. I stopped a long time ago when I realized that days like that were just another form of transition. Any type of transition—whether it is a special day, going from quiet time to bedtime, having to make a sudden trip out of town, going to the store, starting a new school or job, or even something we take for granted like rearranging the furniture (a transition because it's a change in the environment)— all of these should be handled the same way. You must build up to it proactively.

For example, let's say it's grocery shopping day. You look at your watch and say, "I might as well go and get this over with. Now is as good a time as any. Come on, kids. We're going to the store now." At which point the power struggle begins as you nag your kids to hurry up and get ready and they do everything but. Then you start to get aggravated and may even begin to yell at them. By the time you all get in the car, you are extremely agitated and start mumbling things under your breath like "Why didn't I listen to my mother and stay in school? Why did I get married? Why did I have children? Why can't I just go to the store like every-one else?" You stop only because you need to break up a fight in the back seat while simultaneously trying to pull into a parking space at the store. Does this sound familiar?

By planning proactively you can turn this situation around. The evening before you go to the store, maybe at dinnertime, announce, "Tomorrow after we eat lunch we need to go to the grocery store. Is there anything you think we should add to the list?" Then at bedtime say, "Jamie, do you remember what we talked about doing after lunch tomorrow?" If he does, great. If not, you repeat, "We're going to go to the store tomorrow after lunch. What are we going to do? . . . Great, glad you heard me." The next morning at breakfast announce, "Who remembers what we're doing after lunch today?" and respond just as you did the previous evening. Midway through the morning, do it again. At lunchtime, do it again! Also, discuss what getting ready to go looks like: "As soon as we clean up, we need to get our coats on. What do we need to do? Great, glad you heard me." As you are cleaning up lunch, reiterate what getting ready looks like: "You need to get your coat. . . . What should you be doing right now? Getting ready, that's right!" This time when you're in the car you won't be agitated, and you can use positive encouragement by saying, "Wow, you guys were ready to go, and I didn't have to raise my voice either. Thank you. I really appreciate your help."

Proactive planning eliminates reactive behavior, both the child's and yours. If, during the day, you expect any type of transition or any change in the day's normal structure, you have to prepare for it. And any long block of time that is not structured at all—for example, weekends and summer vacations—has to be prepared for. At these times especially things can get really difficult for the child with AD/HD, and when things are challenging for the child, they're going to be challenging for family. You can lessen difficulties during these times by planning ahead proactively. Some things to help you structure weekends and vacations are planned activities or outings, local play groups, team sports, activities through your local parks and recreation department, youth groups or clubs, activities with friends, and a set family game time or playtime. These are just a few suggestions that come to mind. Remember, however, that this doesn't mean structuring every waking moment of your child's day. Kids need to have free time every day.

Here are some examples of things I do with my own family: Saturday night is family campout night—my kind of camping, at least! Every Saturday night that we can, we get our blankets and pillows, make some popcorn, and choose a video. Then we "camp out" in the family room. Sometimes we even roast marshmallows in the fireplace. The kids like it because it's something different. They can stay up late, and we can all talk and be silly. It's something to look forward to. And it's a privilege that can be taken away if they choose to behave inappropriately during the day.

During the summer we have daily activities, if everyone's schedule allows. Once a week we go to the library, and usually twice a week we go swimming for several hours. The kids also take part in theater camp and biweekly ball games. Those are the main things that we do, as far as structuring goes for summertime. Just four things—that's all the proactive planning that's needed. Preparing for summer vacation does not have to be overwhelming.

It's just another type of transition. So, whether it is going from one activity to another, changing classes, coming to the dinner table, going to the store, or even surviving summer vacation, it's a transition. You have to prepare for it.

DON'T GET WORDY

When you are trying to get an idea across to your child, keep the conversation short and simple—don't get wordy! Your child will get lost in the words if you do. Keep it short, simple, clear, and concise. This was probably one of the most challenging things for me to change because I never realized the importance or the impact of language. I'd say things like "Stop it! You know you're not supposed to jump on furniture!" and get the response, "Huh? What?" In the time it had taken me to complete my statement, my child had already moved on to something else and had no idea what I was talking about. She not only felt clueless as to what I had said, but also more than likely a little guilty because of the tone of voice I had used. By the time she processed "Mom's talking to me" in her head, she was too late to grasp the words that were being said but was undoubtedly able to pick up on the tone. Before you talk to your child, you need to stop and think, "Am I saying this in a way that's going to be clear to her? What's my tone of voice? What's my intent in making this statement?" It's really not that difficult. Just pause before you speak; your thoughts will come out much clearer and you will be less likely to ramble. It also allows you to put things positively rather than negatively.

You may have noticed that in the example I gave earlier of going to the store, along with being proactive I used the tool of *verbal feedback*. Verbal feedback involves having the child repeat back to you what he heard you say. In chapter 1 I spoke of learning through our five senses. Using verbal feedback is another way to do this—it teaches the child to fine tune his sense of hearing. He hears not only your message; he hears himself say it back to you. Thus it becomes more concrete for him. Choose your words carefully, though, or the child may end up saying to himself, "What do you think, I'm stupid? I heard what you said." For instance, use phrases like "Sometimes I don't know if what I said comes out clearly. Could you tell me what you heard me say?" or "It helps me to know what I sound like if you tell me what you heard." Eventually you and the child become so used to this pattern of conversation that you can simply and gently say, "Please tell me what you heard me say." You can utilize verbal feedback in a great many situations: during each step of teaching a new task, when giving instructions, or when checking comprehension so you know your child heard you. As with any tool, though, remember not to go overboard with it. This is not about "Hi, Johnny! How are you? Tell me what I just said!" That would be absurd, let alone annoying. Use this tool carefully and at the appropriate times; otherwise it won't be effective.

The following chart gives some examples of verbal feedback. It includes ineffective statements, the changes that need to be made to those statements, and the effective way to make those statements. Please note that words in all capitals indicate shouting or a loud voice, and the ellipses (. . .) indicate pauses for communication purposes.

Whenever you address a child who has AD/HD, and especially when she is in transition from one activity to another, it's important to remember to do the following three things: touch her gently on the arm or shoulder, maintain eye contact, and use verbal feedback. Place your hand gently on her. Resist the temptation to rub or massage her arm or shoulder at this time. Some people with AD/HD are hypersensitive to touch, and to do this would be like winding up a clock—it would distract them when you're trying to get them to focus. You need to maintain eye contact. If the child looks away while you are speaking, wait until she is looking at you again. You may even need to follow her movements and physically

VERBAL FEEDBACK

Ineffective Statement	What to Change	Effective Statement
"BE QUIET! SHHHHH!"	Change wording and tone.	"Please use your inside voice" or "You need to speak softer."
"WHAT DO YOU THINK YOU'RE DOING?"	Change wording and tone.	"What should you be doing right now?" or "Where should you be right now?"
"STOP IT!"	Change wording and tone.	"You need to stop" or "I need for you to stop now. Thank you."
"DID YOU HEAR WHAT I SAID? PAY ATTENTION!"	Change wording and tone.	"Please tell me what you heard me say."
"YOU NEED TO START YOUR HOMEWORK NOW!"	Change tone and gently guide.	"You need to start your homework now. Thanks."
"We're leaving now, OK?"	Tone is good; give count-down and drop the "OK."	"We need to leave in ten minutes.... We're leaving in five minutes; is your coat on? ... We need to go now."
"Susie, go and get me a dish, a spoon, and some pasta. And then finish your homework before you watch TV. Don't forget about the garbage tonight."	Too much information. State only one directive at a time. When that action is completed, state the next.	"Susie, I need you to go to the cupboard and get a dinner plate for me. ... Thanks.... Please hand me a spoon.... Thanks.... Please pass the pasta.... Thanks.... You need to finish your homework before TV.... Tonight is garbage night. Do you remember what you need to do?"
"WHERE HAVE YOU BEEN? YOU'RE LATE!"	Change wording and tone.	"Are you OK? ... When you're late, I worry.... What should you do the next time you're late? ...Thanks."

stay in her face until you're done speaking. Finally, follow up with verbal feedback. The reason for utilizing all three things gets back to the five senses. In using touch, eye contact, and verbal feedback you have engaged three of the five senses. And the more senses you can cover with the same type of information, the more concrete the information will become to the child. Just hearing you say something isn't enough for her because you've covered only one out of five senses.

Be prepared to take the time that is needed to ensure that your child understands every aspect of a new procedure. If a child has never made his bed before and you just tell him to make his bed and expect him to understand and do it right, you may be setting yourself up for frustration. It's better to go through the motions with your child, breaking the task into smaller steps and not going to step two until he is successful with step one. In the making-the-bed example it would look like this: Start by taking the child into his bedroom and explaining, "Today we're going to make the bed together." Show him how to take all the covers off and make the bottom sheet smooth; verbalize as you do this: "Those blankets made a thud sound when I dropped them on the floor. I need to make my hands very flat while I run them over this sheet. Now it's your turn." Then place the covers back on and ask him to do what you did. Did you notice how many senses I covered in that last description? Three—first, he heard me speaking and the sound of the blankets dropping; second, he saw me demonstrate each step and on his turn saw the wrinkles come out of the sheet; and third, I described my hand movements and, on his turn, he felt the sheet smoothing out. Obviously, this example applies to a small child. The great thing about a multisensory method, though, is that it works with any age child. It's a great way to teach an older child to weed the garden, mow the lawn, wash the car, and even cook a dish.

There's another reason to use touch with a child who has AD/HD. You may need to guide the child through the transition from one activity to the next. In this way you are structuring the situation by physically directing her and beginning her transitional movement with her. Again, this is about guiding, not dragging or pushing. There is a difference.

Another communication rule that applies to this child, or any child for that matter, is NEVER to ask a yes-or-no question unless you want a yes-or-no answer. Instead, give options that you both can live with. This is called "giving a voice and a choice," and it's a very effective way to eliminate power struggles.

COMPLETE STEP ONE BEFORE STARTING STEP TWO

Another rule to remember: Never go to step two until you successfully complete step one. In order to complete a task or achieve a goal we have to go through the necessary steps. But these steps may be too challenging for a child with AD/HD, so we have to break them down to even smaller, less challenging steps. Thus, we eliminate some frustrations for the child. He then doesn't feel pressured to go on to the next step. It gets back to the idea of setting him up for success rather than failure. When he feels he has failed he is not going to want to go on to the next step.

The following dialogue illustrates this idea. Realize that the techniques in this example are put in terms of working with a very young child. However, they are adaptable to any age person and to just about any type of situation, whatever the task being learned may be. In this scenario, Mom is in a hurry to leave, but first, Susie needs to get her shoes tied.

> Mom: Come on, Susie. We need to get going; get your shoes tied. (Waiting impatiently)

> Susie: OK! (Fumbling with laces, getting extremely frustrated)

Mom: Here, watch out. Let me just do it.
(Annoyed) There. Let's go.

Susie: (Sounding rather defeated) I tried!

There are actually a couple of things to note about this interaction. First of all, it's an opportunity known as a *teachable moment*—that is, it's an opportunity to teach something. Second, Mom is missing the point that, though Susie knows how to start the process of tying her shoes, she just hasn't mastered the entire process. Mom is expecting her to complete the entire task when it's clear that she can't get past step one. Let's take a look at how this interaction could be made much more effective.

Mom: Susie, we need to leave in five minutes. You need to start putting your shoes on. (Guides Susie to her shoes and stands in the background, putting her own shoes on and watching Susie start to put hers on.)

Susie: (Attempting to tie her shoes, but starting to fumble)

Mom: (Senses Susie is becoming frustrated, calmly places her hands on the laces.) Good job. You got them crossed today! Tomorrow we can practice the bunny ears. So, are you taking a book to read today? (Changes the topic in order to redirect her attention.)

The point of this is to take things one step at a time and to break down big steps into smaller steps, thus making them more attainable goals. The next step in this scenario would involve practicing the next step of shoelace tying with the child when she is in a symptom-controlled state—in other words, when she is calm and not in the middle of a crisis. Again, this may sound simplistic because it's an example of a very young child. The fact is, though, that this is the same process one would use to teach any age child with AD/HD a new task, from mowing the lawn to washing the kitchen floor to driving a car. Whatever the task at hand, it must be broken down into smaller steps.

THEY KNOW NO BOUNDARIES

Boundaries of all types—physical, environmental, and emotional—must be clearly defined for most people with AD/HD. Quite simply, they know no boundaries. Many times they are unaware that their bodies have gone out of bounds. Thus, we actually have to define this for them. Maria Montessori referred to this as "defining their psychic sphere." Often a child with AD/HD cannot walk down a row of desks in a classroom without his hands accidentally hitting people or their work. Or at home, he can't seem to walk from the family room to the kitchen without nudging the cat, bumping his sister on the head, and nearly knocking a plant over. Is he doing this intentionally? No, probably not, and for the most part he doesn't realize to what extent it's affecting others. If it's a problematic behavior, it's up to us to point this out, or define what the boundaries need to be. When he's in a symptom-controlled state you would sit with him and explain to him what you've observed. For example:

> Billy, I've noticed that when you walk through the
> family room you seem to bump into things. I don't
> like yelling at you about it, and I know you don't
> like getting into trouble. So I've got an idea that
> will help us both. When you walk through the
> family room, I need you to keep your hands in
> your pockets or behind your back. Are you willing
> to do that? . . . Great, thanks.

Next time there's a problem it's simply a matter of saying, in a calm voice, "Billy, stop. Where should your hands be?"

So that's a quick introduction to boundaries. They can be an issue in school as well as the home and can include everything from privacy issues to bedtime difficulties to where things belong in the home to, again, physical issues. In this example, I cannot hold the child accountable until I define the problematic behavior, or, in other words, until he is made aware of the behavior and what an effective choice of behavior would be instead. Once that is clear to him, I can then hold him accountable if he chooses not to behave effectively. Regarding environmental boundaries, you have to define what can be done or not done in certain areas of the home. This idea will be discussed in greater detail in the next chapter.

All in the AD/HD Family: Dealing Successfully with Stress

J'm sure that if you're like most parents, you've read some childrearing books. These books offer wonderful information, and the one point they all seem to agree on is that parenting is tough work. It's even tougher when you get thrown the curve of a child with AD/HD. You know how challenging these children can be, especially if you have other children who do not have AD/HD. Often in today's family both parents work, either inside or outside the home, and days are planned with no minutes to spare. Because of all the transitions that go on in our everyday lives, it can be difficult to keep things on an even keel, physically and emotionally, within the family. Add to this whirlwind the AD/HD element—that is, a little forgetfulness, some sloppiness, a dash of disorganization, and, for some of us, a large dose of defiance—and talk about frustrating! Just getting through the day is like running an obstacle course. We've got to do this, then that; be here, but also be there; and, oh yes, be a parent, too. It can be physically and emotionally draining just surviving daily life. But unless we take care of ourselves as parents and caretakers of these children, we won't be able to deal successfully with them.

PERFECT PARENT WANNABE

There is no such thing as a perfect person, let alone a perfect parent. Anyone who tries to tell you differently or prove otherwise is living an obsessive illusion. You may know parents who try to be perfect—one of them may even be you. You know the type: The house is spotless, each parent is involved in several organizations for the betterment of humankind, the kids are well-behaved and involved in every school activity possible, seven-course meals get made every night, and all the children's clothes are homemade. Sometimes not just one, but both parents hold down full-time jobs outside of the home. Whew! That was exhausting just listing all of those accomplishments; think of how exhausting it would be to actually do them.

They sound like wonderful people, don't they? They probably are. What I'd like to know, though, is when do Ozzie and Harriet have time for themselves, not to mention their marriage and relationships with others? I don't advocate being a slob, but I do believe in having realistic expectations. My house may not be spotless, but at least you don't have to worry about creasing the furniture. I decided a long time ago what my priorities were, and I still live by those priorities: myself, my family, my work, my house, my yard, and my outside activities. Reading a story to my children takes precedence over the dishes. This doesn't mean that I avoid household chores. They get done. The dishes can wait another twenty minutes, but I'll never get back that twenty minutes with my kids.

Having realistic expectations is especially important when you are working on behavior management with your child. Having a perfect house doesn't really matter if your kids are out of control. Again, you need to work with one behavior at a time. You'll be overwhelmed if you try to create a "perfect child" and a "perfect house." I say "try" because, in reality, there is no such thing as a perfect child or a perfect house.

It's a good idea to establish a routine or schedule for yourself and try to stick to it as much as possible. In it include time for yourself, your spouse, your children, your job, your housework, and your outside activities. Set priorities and goals, and live by them. As I'm writing this book, I often find myself reminiscing about my own parents and parenting styles of thirty years ago. I look to my right and see my Franklin Planner (a calendar-type planning book). Not a day goes by that I don't refer to it. If it's not written in that book, I don't have to worry about it or plan on doing it. I spend probably twenty minutes a day writing in it, arranging my plans, priorities, and work. How society has changed! I can't remember either of my parents having one, although Mom had a large calendar on her desk, and she used it for the same purpose. Our world and our lives are so much busier today. I wouldn't think of leaving my house without my planner; back then all a woman had to remember was her purse!

My point is this: In order to be successful in today's world and family, we have to take twenty minutes or more just to get our daily priorities and goals organized. If we don't, frustration creeps into our lives, disguised as stress and disorganization. I can't parent exactly as my parents did because the society that we live in today is so much different than theirs. In today's world, we actually have to make time to relax. Otherwise, our frustration level builds and we wonder why we have stress in our lives. It's because we didn't prioritize and set goals. Thirty years ago, time management wasn't thought of in relationship to parenting and running a family. But today, in a family blessed with a child who has AD/HD, time management is a necessity. It goes back to the idea of creating structure and routine, not only for our children, but also for ourselves. Life becomes much more manageable when we can do this.

THE CYCLE OF PARENTAL STRESSES

What are the effects of this disorder on the family unit? AD/HD affects not only the person with the disorder but also everyone in her life. It affects parents (both individually and as a parenting team), siblings, extended family, and friends. We all have to deal with the conflicts and confrontations that arise inside and outside the home as a result of the child's behavior. For some of us, the feelings of anger, shame, and embarrassment are very familiar. We've been asked not to come back to a play group; we've been embarrassed in a store when our child throws a tantrum or starts running around; we've tried to get a baby-sitter and been turned down by family because he's "too hard to handle." And this is not to mention the wonderful experiences of the teenage years.

In addressing a parent group, Dr. John Taylor said, "As the parent of an AD/HD child, you have the distinction of being a member of the most misunderstood, overburdened, and the most under-helped group in the world. The emotional stresses you face are beyond what most people can comprehend. They represent strange contortions and twistings of your psyche and clashes of basic sensibilities such as wanting to love and protect your child, yet feeling incredible rage against your child's behavior." I think that pretty well sums up how it feels to parent these children.

Before I discuss how the family copes with a child who has AD/HD, I need to address some of the stressors that affect parents individually and are causing more stressful situations to arise, adding fuel to the fire. I say this because one stressor can and does lead to another. By dealing with these stressors, however, we can stop this cycle from continuing and, as a result, become more peaceful people and more effective parents. If we take care of ourselves first, we'll be capable of working with others successfully.

In the following figure you can see the stressors that we most commonly encounter: feeling misunderstood, guilty and inadequate, overinvolved, angry, and emotionally bankrupt. It's fairly obvious why we would feel misunderstood. Unless you've actually lived life as the parent of a child with AD/HD you have no idea what it's like. It's easy to see why others would have a hard time relating. We hear things like "You don't discipline correctly" and "It's all your fault." This is false. The truth is that, although we probably could use some help disciplining, it is NOT OUR FAULT. We are not the cause. We get judged by just about everyone for just about everything. It's a catch-22: If I assume that my child's normal, then I'm a failure as a parent; if I recognize his handicap and try to deal with it logically, then I'm an overprotective parent; if I wear out and lose control of him, then I'm overpermissive. Talk about confusing!

It gets even more confusing when we seek professional help. We're told, "It's just a phase; he's just an active and creative boy with a vivid imagination." Or the best one: "He's all right, but you and your family are the problem." This leaves us frustrated and confused, doubting whether professionals can really help.

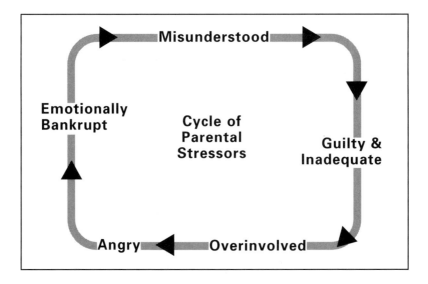

The judgments and ignorance of others become even more apparent after an accurate diagnosis. Then you hear opinions like "There's no such thing as AD/HD," or "He's not that bad," or "You're just trying to cover up for being a bad parent." If you choose medication as a treatment option it gets even worse—then you're addicting him to drugs or you're sedating him. You can fend off all of this ignorance by responding with accurate information about AD/HD and your child. Obviously, these people need more information, and, if they truly want to help, it's worth it to share some of your information with them. If they become interfering, thank them for their concern and remind them that you are well aware of all of the circumstances and issues that are present and have already thought them through. Remind them also that the bottom line is what's best for the child and that, at this moment, this course of treatment is what's best. Above all, you need not lose your self-respect over their opinions; you know what you are doing. Others' opinions of you should not concern you. You will more than likely hear these kinds of things again in the future. The trick is to detach from the conversation, physically and emotionally, and to do it as quickly as possible—you can say, for instance, "Thanks for caring, but I'm handling it."

After these things take hold, we enter into the next phase of the cycle, feeling guilty and inadequate. This is where you say to yourself, "I'm not trying hard enough." This is the phase where we've been duped into believing the judgmental and ignorant comments of others, so much so that at times we don't need others to tell us these things anymore because we've now learned to self-medicate with criticism—that is, to put ourselves down. We can do a very good job of beating ourselves up, thank you.

Remember, expectations are nothing more than premeditated resentments. We have expectations of what a good parent should be like, and when we fall short we end up being resentful. We resent our child and then feel guilty over the resentment. What parents don't realize is that resentment is a natural consequence of raising a child with AD/HD and that they don't need to feel guilty about it. It's also natural to feel overwhelmed. But just because we feel inadequate at times doesn't mean we are incapable of parenting. It's very easy for us to be overcome by our negative feelings and leave the positive feelings by the wayside. We need to remember, though, that once a solid bond of love is established, it's always there no matter what negative feelings come up. Know that it's OK to feel resentful every now and then. If you find that your resentments are occurring more often than that, you may want to take a close look at your expectations of both yourself and your child. Are they realistic, or maybe a little unrealistic? You may want to take some time to reevaluate your priorities.

As a result of trying to compensate for the guilt and our concern for the difficulties these kids may be experiencing, we have a habit of becoming enmeshed in the need to protect them and meet their constant needs. We become overly involved. Not only is this draining for us as parents, it also makes it difficult for everyone in the immediate family. Siblings become very jealous. The overinvolvement shows up in different ways. For one, parents have the need to intervene to protect their child. But when you restrict your child from taking risks because of potential consequences, you are denying her the opportunity to learn to cope with responsibility and difficulty. In doing this you don't go to the opposite extreme, so that all your child encounters are failures. You find a middle ground, one where she can be successful and realize she is responsible for that success.

Another way we get overly involved is when we nag. Contrary to what your parents probably showed you, you do not have to nag to be a good parent—or partner for that matter. When you continually badger another person, you might as well be saying, "Please ignore 80 percent of what I have said because I'll say it again!" It is the most common error we make as parents. We are likely, especially on difficult tasks, to want to intervene and "help." It's only natural knowing how much assistance these children require, but the tendency is to overdo it. Nagging is like a parental pacifier. We think that since we've told the child to do something, it should get done, thus relieving us from responsibility for the action or blame. But the child's lack of attention and focus, combined with a short memory for verbal messages, leads us into an unending cycle. It begins with continual directives, reminders, commands, and suggestions. Then we gradually lose trust in the child's ability to get anything accomplished without our nagging. So the nagging increases and the child becomes sloppier, slower, and more forgetful. This makes us nag more, and so the cycle goes. Take a look at the number of verbal directives you give and then, instead of nagging the child, focus on making a change in the environment that supports what it is the child should be doing.

Other types of overinvolvement are the prince/princess syndrome (spoiling her rotten), the "Oh, poor baby" syndrome (pitying her), and the "Here, let me do that for you" syndrome (babying). I remember a funny story about the "Oh, poor baby" syndrome. I knew a couple who had a child with AD/HD back in the 1970s, when we were still trying to figure out this disorder. The boy would often get into trouble, and when the father would start to discipline him, the mother would intervene, saying, "Leave him alone. He's just coming down with something." This went on for years. The child grew older, and the mother still resorted to this intervention. Finally, on one such occasion, after hearing her comment the father exploded, "He's been coming down with something for ten years now! Isn't he over it yet?"

All of these forms of overinvolvement discourage the child from developing normal social skills. They can leave him socially and emotionally immature, thinking that the world is an overwhelming place that requires constant adult intervention in order to be successful. But he didn't learn to walk by your doing the walking for him. He can learn a lot more from being occasionally unsuccessful at something than he can by watching you be continually successful.

To cut down on overinvolvement, encourage your child's efforts. Be concerned and involved, but don't overdo it. Personal strength comes from practice and persistence and from accepting life's challenges. Encourage this development in your child and in yourself. Learn to be grateful for each step she takes toward achieving a goal. Give help but don't serve excessively. And there are ways to reduce frustration without denying her the opportunity to learn to face challenging situations. If you are already overinvolved, be prepared to deal with your child's attempts to manipulate you and keep the status quo. When she says, "If you were a good mom you would do this for me," be strong and do the opposite.

Anger is a common, potentially dangerous emotional stressor in a family. You love your child, you hate him, and you beat yourself up with guilt for not being a better parent. You've tried everything to get through to the child, and it's frustrating the heck out of you. So what do you do? You get angry. In addressing that same parent group, John Taylor said, "Put love, hate, guilt into a blender and put it on high speed—this is how parents feel inside." As parents of these children, we have a lot to feel angry about.

A potentially dangerous emotion, anger has to be dealt with. First of all, don't put the responsibility for your anger on somebody else, especially your child. Blaming someone else is like saying, "I love you because you made me be in love with you." Wrong—you love someone because of a feeling you have inside. It's the same with anger: It's not the person; it's the feeling inside. Think of it like this: "I'm getting angry as I listen to you," not "You're making me so angry by what you're saying." When you accept that your anger comes from inside of you, it puts it under your control.

Next, differentiate between embarrassment and anger. For example, when your child starts to misbehave in public, you probably think to yourself, "I could just crawl under a rock." But if you recognize that the primary feeling here is one of embarrassment, not anger, you can then focus on preventing the embarrassment instead of the anger. Remind yourself that your embarrassment is needless and more than likely excessive, that it's him and not you who's creating the distraction, and that not getting upset about it is a lot more important than what a bunch of strangers think.

Differentiate between the child and the disorder. Remember that AD/HD is the bad guy here, not your child. It's like when my daughter had the chicken pox. I loved her, but I really hated all those red spots. Think of AD/HD as those ugly red spots. Understand that AD/HD is the source of the negative feelings you may be having, not your child.

Remember that everyone has problems in life (or, as my mother says, everyone has a cross to bear). There is no particular injustice in the fact that you have been chosen to deal with AD/HD. It's pointless to continually ask, "Why me?" How could this happen to you? Very easily—because it has.

The last stressor I will talk about is feeling emotionally bankrupt. This is when you end up feeling completely defeated and drained. Basically, you're at the end of your rope. You have come to the realization that no ordinary parenting technique is applicable in its purest form to AD/HD. A tragic reaction in this stage is child abuse—verbal, emotional, physical, or sexual. If you're at the end of your rope, it's best to separate yourself from the child. Take a break or a vacation and physically remove yourself from the child's environment. What you need at this stage is to regain your emotional balance. Talk to someone who is supportive and does understand, otherwise you'll be starting the cycle of stressors all over again with feeling misunderstood. Dealing with emotional bankruptcy can be very difficult and is next to impossible to do on your own. If you are at this stage it is a good idea to get some professional help.

Preventing emotional bankruptcy is much easier than having to deal with it head on. You can prevent it by learning to get rid of your need to control your child's behavior. There is only one person on this earth whom you can control, and that's YOU. So concentrate on getting control of your own emotional reactions to your child's behavior, rather than controlling your child.

Lessen stresses by stopping them early. Calmly and firmly set limits. Make a clear and simple statement that the child is crossing your boundaries and that you want her to stop now. And then back it up with a firm, silent, and somewhat dramatic action that shows you mean what you say. Your intention is to not allow her behavior to continue. I've drawn up a seven-point list called Countering Stressors. You can use this for a quick reference when you're feeling stressed.

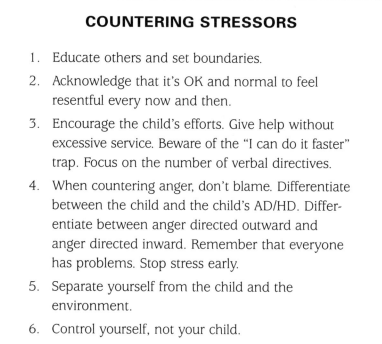

COUNTERING STRESSORS

1. Educate others and set boundaries.

2. Acknowledge that it's OK and normal to feel resentful every now and then.

3. Encourage the child's efforts. Give help without excessive service. Beware of the "I can do it faster" trap. Focus on the number of verbal directives.

4. When countering anger, don't blame. Differentiate between the child and the child's AD/HD. Differentiate between anger directed outward and anger directed inward. Remember that everyone has problems. Stop stress early.

5. Separate yourself from the child and the environment.

6. Control yourself, not your child.

7. Get professional help.

CHANGING YOUR OWN BEHAVIOR

The biggest factor in eliminating frustration and changing your child's behavior is changing your own behavior. If you want your child to behave differently, you need to behave differently. Your approach to parenting has to change. You must get rid of the old negative tools and discover and utilize positive tools. That means replacing nagging, yelling, and punishing with tools like encouragement, redirection, and positive reinforcement.

Positive tools are really quite simple and encompass a variety of approaches. Here are three to start with.

Acknowledgment

This is as simple as saying, "Thanks, I really appreciate that" or "Good job!" Find times and reasons throughout each day to acknowledge the small things as well as the big things. This may be tricky at first because, again, we're so used to pointing out weaknesses. Acknowledge a task even if it isn't completed perfectly; comment only on the part that was done correctly. Even acknowledge attempts and then ask if the child would like a (supportive) suggestion on how to get the rest of the task done. Another form of acknowledgment is gratitude. I can remember at Thanksgiving instead of saying the usual prayer before dinner, we would, as a family, take turns saying what we were grateful for. I got to wondering why this could only happen one day a year. Why not every day? Believe it or not, you can find something good in every day. So sometimes now instead of the usual prayer, we'll each say what we're grateful for. And each day when I pick my children up from school I ask what the best part of their day was. Another tool is "love envelopes"—envelopes in which you put messages of love or encouragement. This is a good way to acknowledge someone when you might have forgotten to. The message can be something like "Good job at school today" or "Thanks for getting the lawn mowed" or even just "Love you!" And these aren't just for the kids; Mom and Dad need an envelope, too.

Time for Play

Here's your chance to lighten up! Besides the fact that it's important to relax and have some fun with your kids, play serves as a learning process. Among the things learned in play are social skills, attitudes toward interpersonal relationships, communication skills, cooperation, and mutual respect. These are all especially important to the child with AD/HD. You may want to keep in mind the difference between competitive and cooperative games. In a competitive game, two opposing factors, or teams, work against each other to achieve a goal that only one team can obtain. In a cooperative game, players work together to achieve a goal that all can obtain. Many times it's somewhat difficult for kids with AD/HD to take part in competitive games. They require greater focusing capability, and the frustration factor is higher. You may want to introduce them gradually to competition by starting with cooperative games. You can adapt most games to meet this goal, whether they are board games or games involving physical activity. Something else you can do as a family is to make everyday happenings into a team effort—from cleaning the house to yard work to planning a family vacation or event to building or putting something together.

Special Time

Lasting anywhere from an hour to an entire day, special time can be planned around a particular event or happen "just because." One example is one-on-one time, the opportunity for each parent to spend time alone with each child. We call it "date night" in our house. It doesn't have to be anything outrageous—simply going for a walk together is great. Another type of special time is what we like to call King/Queen for a Day. This is a day for one person to be free to do just about anything, including being free from obligations and the usual responsibilities, such as chores.

SINGLE PARENTING

Another stressor in today's society, single parenting, can be overwhelming whether or not your child has AD/HD. The difference here is that you may feel your frustrations to be somewhat more intense, and rightly so. Though it sounds a bit clichéd, things will get better over time. In time we become more comfortable with our role as a single parent and, gradually, as our confidence grows, the pieces of the puzzle begin to fall back into place. All of the techniques discussed in this book are applicable to any parent, whether he or she has a spouse or not.

Of great benefit for all parents, but especially single parents, is the idea of networking. Networking is a fancy, high-tech way of saying talking about things and developing a good support system. You have already begun to network by reading this book, and you can continue by finding others in your situation. You can eliminate stressors in your life by talking and listening to someone who's "been there and done that," someone who can relate to you without judging you. Networking has other benefits, too—for example, helping you find reliable child care, whether it's a baby-sitter for Saturday night, a day care provider, or a friend or relative who's willing to take your child on short notice. You can create a child care network of sorts by exchanging child care with a friend—one day a week you can watch his children and another day he can watch yours.

Another thing that helps you as a single parent is to proactively rearrange your day to make the most of your time. Remember, also, to avoid being distracted or enmeshed in trivial problems. In other words, don't sweat the small stuff, and choose your battles. One of the most important things you can do is to take care of yourself and your needs. A key aspect of becoming a better parent is developing yourself as a whole person. When your needs are being met, it's much easier to meet the needs of others in your life, especially your children. Arrange as balanced a life as possible. Make sure to set aside some time for yourself and just yourself every day. It may sound kind of insignificant, but it's not. It's incredibly beneficial.

Communicating with a former spouse about your child can be challenging. He or she may not be supportive or agree with how you feel the child needs to be parented, including the treatment program. Let's face it. If this person wasn't supportive of you when you were a couple, why in the world would you expect him or her to be supportive of you now? On the other hand, you may need to look at your expectations. Sometimes the best plan is to accept the other person just the way that person is and get rid of any resentments you're harboring because they're getting in the way of effective communication. And that's not only harming you, but also your child. Limit communication, keeping it businesslike and courteous, short and sweet. If the ex-spouse chooses not to follow the treatment program when the child is there, then so be it; it's not your choice. Let nature take its course, and eventually some symptomatic behaviors will make themselves evident when the child is in the ex-spouse's care. True, you and your child will be the ones paying the price for the other parent's choices. Focus a hundred percent on treatment when the child is with you.

If you are fortunate enough to have an amicable relationship with your ex-spouse, talk it over and find out what his or her concerns are regarding treatment. Those concerns, whether or not they are based in fact, are very real. Hear your ex-spouse out respectfully, acknowledge his or her concerns, and state your own concerns and rationale. In so doing you may be able to share some unknown information and shed some light for each other.

EFFECTS ON PARENTS' RELATIONSHIP

When was the last time you and your spouse spent an evening alone, just the two of you? Do you remember what you talked about? I'll bet it was your child or children. Just as you need to take care of yourselves individually, it's also important to take care of yourselves as a couple, to give your relationship some attention. Here's the challenging part: See if you can spend time together without talking about your child. Do whatever you have to do to shift your focus onto something else. Do something that keeps you actively involved in the moment: bowling, watching a movie, canoeing, white-water rafting, sky diving—whatever it takes. Or spend some time with people who don't have children; the weird looks they give you when you attempt to talk about junior's latest escapade will put a quick end to that topic.

When it *is* an appropriate time to talk about your child's latest escapade, a common issue for parents is how to deal with it. I've found that parents don't always see eye to eye on how to handle a child with AD/HD, and many times they have very different expectations. This can be remedied via effective communication, negotiation, and compromise. Remember, you are both on the same team; you both want what's best for the child and the entire family. If you start to blame, shame, or manipulate your spouse into doing things your way, you will more than likely put your partner on the defensive. When you're on the same team, this is not a very effective way to achieve a goal.

For example, take this conversation between Betty and Bill. Betty wants to talk to Bill about their son, Aaron. Aaron and Bill have not been getting along well for quite some time. Betty sees that this is not healthy and wants to make things different so that they all can get along better. Bill is at the kitchen table reading the newspaper, and Betty brings her coffee in and joins him.

Betty:	Bill, put down that paper. We need to talk. (Her tone is very demanding.)
Bill:	(Lowers paper slightly, but still glances at it.)
Betty:	Aaron is very upset with you because you scold him too much. If you weren't so selfish you would spend more time with him. He's fine with me; it's just you. (Stated in a very judgmental tone.)
Bill:	Well, I . . .
Betty:	Don't even try to deny it. You know it's true.

Bill: (Raises paper back up and speaks
in a resentful tone.) Whatever.

Betty walks away from the table and wonders why she and Bill don't seem to talk much anymore. Could it be that she was and is blaming, shaming, and manipulating? In a nutshell ... YES. Right now Bill is left feeling like his thoughts and feelings don't count; he's feeling defeated, frustrated, and defensive. When someone beats you up with words it makes you want to fight back and make your point known. Betty needs to realize this and understand that when you present yourself as a know-it-all you need to be prepared to do it all, too. Effective communication should not make the other person feel defensive or angry. Let's see what effective communication looks like using the same scenario with Betty and Bill.

Betty: (Touching Bill lightly on the shoulder)
Bill, I need to talk with you. Is now a
good time?

Bill: Well, I'm reading right now.
Maybe later.

Betty: (Calmly) OK. Which would be better for
you, in twenty minutes or in an hour?

Bill: An hour is good.

Betty: Thanks.

One hour later . . .

Betty: (Touching Bill's shoulder, in a calm
voice) It's an hour later now; remember
we said we'd talk now.

Bill: (Putting paper aside) OK, what did
you want to talk about?

Betty: Thanks for being willing to talk with me
about this. I've noticed that you and

Aaron have been arguing a lot lately. I
would like to hear what's going on for
you and see if we can work out a plan
for you and Aaron to communicate
more effectively. Will that work for you?

Betty has opened the door to effective communication. She
used "I" statements to describe her observations in terms of her
own feelings and perceptions, she used a problem-solving approach,
and she focused on feelings. Consequently, Bill has no need to feel
defensive; he knows his feelings on the matter are important and
worth being heard. Now they are both working toward the same
goal and are on the same team to achieve that goal.

EXTENDED FAMILY

Having the support of your extended family and friends is a
huge help when raising a child who has AD/HD. When you don't
have this, however, it poses an obstacle for you to deal with and
overcome. It helps to keep in mind that family members are acting
out of love for the child in the only way they know how, and more
than likely they have no knowledge of AD/HD or how to deal with
it. Also, they don't have to live with the child on a daily basis (and
if they did, they probably would be more understanding).

When they don't understand about AD/HD, it's easy for these
members of the "outside world" to place blame on the parents. One
reason is that, unlike other challenges children face, AD/HD is not
tangible; it's not a disability they can see. A sad fact in our world is
that if people can't see it, it must not be there. They have to put the
blame on something tangible—parents, the home environment,
schools. It's interesting how they can start by showing concern for
the child and end up judging the parents. "We only want what's
best for her" becomes another way of saying, "You're not doing it
right; if you did it my way you wouldn't have these problems" or

"She never acts like this with me—you're just not doing it right." What's frustrating about this is that your child usually does behave differently with others than she does with you. This can leave you with strong feelings of guilt and inadequacy. What you need to remember here is that, again, you did not cause the problem, and extended family members don't know any better—they are un-informed. Kids with AD/HD do interact differently in different en-vironments.

The judgment I used to hear all the time was "Well, she doesn't act that way with me—you just need to spend more time with her." This used to drive me absolutely bonkers. Then I started observing the situation a little more closely. When my daughter, Ashley, was with me, I was being a mom. I was cooking, cleaning, doing laun-dry, paying bills, and managing a household on a daily basis. And when my daughter would spend the day with Grandma, Grandma would put those things aside for the day and do nothing but spend eight hours one-on-one with the child. Of course a child isn't going to have any difficulties when the adult caretaker is doing nothing but pleasing the child. In real life I don't have the ability or capacity to spend every waking moment serving the needs of my child; I have to maintain a household and manage a career. I am first and foremost a parent, but if these other rituals of daily living don't get handled, I won't be able to be a parent. That's reality.

Another reason children with AD/HD behave differently in dif-ferent environments is the structure of the environment itself. I remember when we were going through the diagnostic process with Ashley. She was almost four years old at the time and enrolled in a Montessori preschool (not the same one where she was told to sit down!). I told her teacher about her disorder and the teacher was a little surprised that we were going through a diagnostic process. She hadn't noticed any outrageous behavioral problems with Ash-ley—and the only thing she could point to was a time she had to ask Ashley to stop climbing on a bookcase. So I did some more observing and realized why this was. The structure of a Montessori classroom is based on the inward structure of the child. The child learns respect for others and respect for the classroom materials. There are literally hundreds of these materials (or "works") and approximately fifty to seventy-five different ones out in a classroom at one time. Once the child has been given a lesson in the works available, she is free to choose among them. Ashley wasn't having difficulties in her classroom because as long as she worked respectfully she could do as many works in a day as she wanted—and many she did! Like the Energizer bunny, she kept going, and going, from one work to the next. In a Montessori classroom this could very easily be taken for enthusiasm for the works, rather than possible AD/HD. But this was a huge lesson for me. I learned that when you proactively structure your child's environment, she can and will thrive with incredible success.

Sometimes extended family and friends may have experienced the child's wild side and can't deal with it. It's frustrating when a member of your own family says, "I can't baby-sit anymore. He's just too much for me." When this happens, accept it and go on. And when you do have to be around this relative with your child, make it for short periods, when you know the child is in a symptom-controlled state (that is, when he's calm and can attend to tasks). If you're having Christmas dinner at Aunt Sally's and you know she always has that antique vase out on her table, call her beforehand and tactfully ask if she wouldn't mind putting it away for the day: "Aunt Sally, I love that vase of yours, and I know you do, too. I'm worried that when we come over, Johnny's going to be tempted to touch it. Though I'll do my best to keep him from it, I can't guarantee that he won't, so I was wondering if, just for that day, you wouldn't mind putting it up." Here's another option: Call Aunt Sally a week beforehand and ask if you and your son can come for a visit. Once there, walk with Johnny around the house, pointing out where he can and cannot be. When you get to the vase, stop. Instruct him that when he's near this vase he needs to keep his hands in his pockets. Ask him to show you what that will look like. Or say, "Let's practice that," and practice it with him. You also need to decide what the consequence will be if he chooses to misbehave. Find a spot in Aunt Sally's house where he can chill out until he's ready to join the family again.

Blame often gets thrown around when the subject of how your child came to have AD/HD comes up. "She's just like her father" or "No one on our side of the family was like this" are common statements. I can remember a day when my daughter was two and decided to see how many holes she could dig in our backyard. We'd intervene and walk away only to turn around and see her doing it again (this was before her diagnosis and treatment). My mother-in-law witnessed this and began to laugh, saying to my husband, "Mark, you are just getting paid back for all the times you did stuff like this when you were a kid." I thought, "Wait a minute—why do I have to be subjected to his 'paybacks'? I didn't do stuff like that." And the truth was I didn't—but my brother did! Since AD/HD is hereditary, someone somewhere on the family tree was probably like this. But it didn't help me—and it won't help you—to blame one side or the other. What matters is that your child is affected by this right now.

Pressure from the outside world can really be annoying. It helps, though, to remember that there is no such thing as a perfect parent. There are only parents who choose constantly to educate themselves and become more knowledgeable in order to become better parents.

Most hurtful comments that come from our extended families are due to their limited knowledge of AD/HD. If they are open to the idea of educating themselves, great! Share all the information you can with them. But if they are not interested, that's OK, too. It's their choice. Accept their decision and change your attitude toward them. You can't make them any different, and they can't make you any different unless you allow them to.

Try to understand where they're coming from, or what their possible motives may be. They may be trying to make up for their past history as a parent. Maybe they haven't forgiven themselves yet for the job they did. Maybe they had no support from anyone. You might let them know that they did the best they could with the knowledge they had and that's all anyone can do. I myself have been put in an interesting position as far as this goes. My parents don't need to change. I do. I choose to go by the saying "Take what you like and leave the rest." I choose how I'm going to respond to them, and whether or not I take their comments to heart is up to me.

Above all else, you are the parent. Take responsibility and be the parent. One of the reasons outsiders say the things they do is because they know it will affect you. Stop letting it get to you. Make the conscious decision not to engage in any potentially harmful conversations. Walk away from them. State that you are not willing to discuss this at this point in time and change the topic of conversation.

SIBLINGS—IT'S NOT FAIR!

"It's not fair!" is a common battle cry in most homes, and it's even more common in a home where a child has AD/HD. My response to it has always been, "You're right. This might not be fair, but I'm doing the best I can." Life is not fair—why teach our children that it is? This doesn't mean that you should expose them to all the cruel realities of the world, but it does mean that if you're trying continually to make everything fair you're going to wear yourself out and give your children false expectations of the world. Parents can easily fall into this trap. Guilt can be a powerful motivator and manipulator. We have a natural desire to want the best for our kids, to be able to give them everything. We've been programmed by society to believe that, by doing this, we create happiness. And we're fooled into believing this by the results of our giving. We give them what they want and then they must be happy because they stop asking; they are content. What we've really just taught our children is to find contentment and happiness in material things or actions—

"Buy me this" or "Take me here." We've taught them that when you make someone miserable enough, that person will give in. The irony of this is that, in a way, we sometimes parent like this. That is, if we make the child miserable enough, via punishment, we think he will change and become "good," when actually all we've taught him is that eventually he's going to have to do it Mom's or Dad's way. We haven't changed any behavior; rather, we have clearly defined what manipulation looks like. That's not the end result we want.

Another fairness issue among siblings and peers is that of privileges. "But Mom…" your child will whine, "it's not fair. Sally gets to go to the park by herself. Why can't I?" Some parents respond to this by initiating a power struggle: "Because I said so, that's why!" Or sometimes when you hear this as a parent you begin to get those guilts again: "Maybe I am too strict. If Sally's mom lets her go, maybe I should let my child go." This is what I refer to as "parental peer pressure." Think about it, though. What do your instincts really tell you? We tend to ignore our instincts in order to conform to society's pressures. But we have them for a reason. They are a tool for survival. So this is not about power over the child or guilt that we're not making the right parenting choices, but rather listening and following our gut instincts. Try saying to your child, "I know you want to go to the park, and I also know how important it is to you to feel like you fit in with all your friends. What I also know is that I'm not ready for you to go to the park on your own yet." This way the child knows that, yes, she probably is capable of handling the situation. The problem is not her, but rather Mom and Dad and what they are ready for. And it's really not so much a problem as it is just a fact. Know also that you've just observed another lesson to start working on and teach your child—how to be safe in the outside world. It's another goal to work toward, and that's what privileges are—goals that have been reached.

There are some privileges that only come with age. For example, you'll hear, "How come she gets to stay up a half hour longer than me? It's not fair!" In all actuality this really is fair, because it's a fact of life. As a child grows into adolescence, he doesn't need as much sleep as he used to. A five-year-old does need more sleep than a ten-year-old—it's just a fact of life. Unfortunately, the facts of life are hard for a child to comprehend. We as adults can understand this, but children don't have that capacity yet. And we all know that children with AD/HD can be a far cry from rational. So how do we work with this type of situation? There are a couple of ways. First, it is a type of transition, so you can work up to it with some planning and forethought. Explain the situation and what it's going to look like before it happens. Second, and this goes back to my earlier comment that life's not fair, simply tell the child, "I understand that you feel this isn't fair, but it's just the way life is," and leave it at that.

You can do a simple exercise with your child to prove this point. You can even do this yourself: On a sheet of paper, number down from 1 through 12. On this list, write twelve things that you like about your life, or even about life in general. They can be anything you like, from your beliefs to material things to your favorite food. It doesn't matter what order you list things in—just write down whatever pops into your head. I'll share mine with you, but please try and think of some of your own.

Things I like about my life:

1. My house

2. My children

3. My job

4. Education

5. Faith, religion

6. Friends

7. Family

8. Computer

9. My car

10. Chocolate

11. Reading

12. Riding my bike

Look at your own list. These are all things you like about your life and that you're glad you have in your life. I hate to tell you this, but none of these things is fair. It's not fair that I have a house because some people are forced to live in cardboard boxes. It's not fair that I have my children because some people who want children are unable to have them. It's not fair that I have my job because some people are unemployed, or they don't like their jobs. It's not fair that I have my education because some people never even get to set foot in school. You get the idea.

This doesn't mean that I should feel guilty about having these things. It simply means that there are things in my life that to others seem unfair, but there are also things in others' lives that seem unfair to me. Someone in Austria may have written out a list like this and included that he likes to go hiking in the Alps. Well, that's not fair because I don't get to do that. Does it mean that he's wrong for having that privilege? No. It's just a fact of that person's life.

Doing this exercise also makes you realize what you do have in life that you may have taken for granted and now can appreciate a little more. When we spend our time and energy trying to rationalize, equalize, and justify the things we have or don't have, it's time and energy wasted. There will always be someone experiencing something we never will. Our time is much better spent recognizing and teaching our children to appreciate what we do have.

INVASION OF PRIVACY

Invasion of privacy is a common issue not just for kids with AD/HD and their siblings, but for all kids, especially adolescents. For some families it involves stealing or even being physically attacked by a child with AD/HD. As parents we do have an obligation to protect our children and their rights as well as our own rights. What this issue really involves is defining boundaries—defining where your child's body may or may not be.

If it's an issue of environmental boundaries, clearly define where the child may or may not go and what she may or may not touch. If the child seems to be curiously attracted to something in your home and you have to worry about her physical safety or that of others if she should touch it (for example, knives, medications, and so on), lock it up. Put it away. If certain things shouldn't be touched because of sentimental or monetary value, put them away also. Gradually, you can reintroduce them into the environment. And I literally mean reintroduce. If your heart is set on having Great Aunt Gerti's antique vase on display, then, when your child is in a symptom-controlled state, introduce her to the vase. I know it sounds silly. But what it's about is clearly defining how she may or may not touch it. Say, for example, the vase is on the dining room table. Susie comes in, sees it, and immediately goes for it. You think to yourself, "Oh, boy. Another opportunity for a learning experience," and you quickly and calmly intervene: "It's a beautiful vase, isn't it? Come sit with me at the table." You gently guide Susie, by touching her shoulder, toward the table. "This vase is very special to me. Do you know why?" and you proceed to explain. "So that's why we look at it only with our eyes and not our hands. Do you under-stand? I don't know if that came out real clear. Could you tell me what you heard me say?"

Or if you don't mind your child's touching an object, but want him to do it in a certain, or respectful, way, be willing to demonstrate that to him: "This is the way you may touch this" or "This is some-thing we need to look at together." If he then abuses that right, put the object away, calmly saying, "You may not touch this like that. I need to put it away for now. We'll try again next week."

Another option is to make it a rule that if an object is special to someone, it should be in his bedroom. This is especially true for siblings. Anything that they don't wanted touched should be in their bedrooms. And bedrooms are private. They are not to be entered without permission. But if an object is not in the bedroom, it's available for anyone to touch in a respectful way. You have just defined a boundary: "Susie's bedroom is hers—you may not go in it without her permission." If this isn't enough, put a lock on the door. This is not to lock the child in, but rather to keep him out. You can install a hook-and-eye lock at the very top of the door. When Susie's not in her room, keep it locked so Johnny doesn't go in.

Rules regarding physical boundaries being crossed need to be clearly defined for everyone. One of those rules is no hitting. No matter how angry someone is, it is not OK to take out that anger on another person. Show your children how they can safely get angry without physically involving others. When the child physically invades someone else's space via hitting, kicking, tripping, spitting, or similar behavior, she needs to go to time-out immediately, with the explanation that the behavior she chose is unacceptable: "When you hit someone it hurts them. You may not hit. It's not acceptable. If you're angry you need to use your words." (I'll discuss time-out and a variant, quieting time, more fully in chapter 7.)

You can use observation to be more proactive about your child's anger. Do angry battles happen after the kids have been together for a certain amount of time? If so, they may need to spend time playing separately, or in separate rooms. Is anger a problem only when you're not in the room? If so, you will need to supervise your children more closely. This doesn't mean becoming a watchdog—just remain close enough so that you can quickly and calmly intervene when necessary. I know firsthand how challenging this can be. There was a time in my life when the simplest things, like taking a shower or throwing a load of wash in, meant strategically planning ahead. They had to be done when the children were sleeping or when I knew that someone else would be there to supervise. Many times I can remember my mother's stopping by for a few minutes and my asking her if she could stay long enough for me to hop into the shower. Mind you, this may have been at 3:00 in the afternoon, but if I hadn't gotten up before the kids did, this was the only way I could get a shower in.

Sometimes kids will feel like their emotional and mental boundaries are being crossed when a sibling with AD/HD invades their space. This is the old embarrassment factor, or "Mom! He's doing it again! Make him leave me and my friends alone!" This is especially true of teenage siblings. No matter how much you try to explain that other people's opinions don't matter, it's still a major concern for them. Our job as parents is to help the siblings understand that they are not responsible for their brother's or sister's actions and that if others judge them on the actions of this child, their opinions are not worth caring about. Teach all the children in the family not to get trapped in the middle. If one person has something to say to another, it needs to be said directly to that person. When Johnny's big sister Susie hears things from her friends like "Gosh, your brother's annoying. He's so loud!" Susie needs to remind her friends to tell Johnny directly, rather than telling her about it. It does her no good to get this information, but it may do Johnny some good to hear it. In this way the sibling makes it clear to others and herself that she is not responsible for her brother's or sister's behavior, or anyone else's behavior for that matter.

Also, it is a good idea to make sure that the sibling has some "protected time" with his friends. This is a time when he can be with his friends and not have to worry about a brother or sister barging in on them. An added benefit of this is that it can also serve as quality one-on-one time for a parent and the child with AD/HD. By doing this you not only remove the child with AD/HD from her sibling's space, thus guaranteeing the sibling some protected time, but you also get to spend some time with her. It's a win-win situation. Mom and Dad should also get some protected time, too. The key is to explain to everyone in the family what this arrangement is going to look like before it happens. That way there is no "flak" from anyone involved, and you all will benefit.

Through observation you will also be able to spot any patterns or triggers between siblings that could proactively be changed or restructured in order to eliminate conflicts. Note what's going on between them and in the environment at the time a flare-up occurs. If you see a potentially troublesome pattern, change it. If you see the need to incorporate a routine, do it. As far as siblings fighting, what matters is not who started it, but rather who's finishing it—you. In a fight, it's usually up to the parent to intervene and redirect all involved to cool down. While they are cooling down, the siblings need to figure out how they could have handled the situation without fighting, what they can do next time, and what they are willing to do to make this a win-win situation. In other words, put them in the same boat. Eventually, they will be able to utilize the tools of successful confrontation.

SUCCESSFUL CONFRONTATION

You may already have heard of successful confrontation. It's a trendy way of saying "getting along together." It may sound trite, but it really does work. A method that I use myself and also teach in my class is a three-step version of successful confrontation. This can be utilized by anyone, anywhere, anytime. And it is just what it sounds like, a successful way to confront someone in order to settle differences. Here are the three steps, with descriptions of how they might apply to a confrontation between a sibling and her brother, who has AD/HD.

1. State the problem: The sibling makes a clear statement to her brother of what is bothering her. "Please stop drawing on my homework."

2. State your want/need: The sibling then makes a clear statement of what she wants her brother to do instead. "Please draw on your

sketch tablet" or "Please ask me for some drawing paper" or "Please go into the living room."

3. State how you'll support the person in this: The sibling makes the deal. "Here's what I'll do for you..." or "I'll support you by..." or "If you do . . . then I'll . . ." By doing this she's seeking a win-win resolution and showing attention to her brother.

Let's take a look at two scenarios involving confrontation, the first with an unsuccessful outcome. Susie is doing her homework at the dining room table and Johnny, who has AD/HD, comes in.

Johnny: Whatcha doin'?

Susie: (Slightly annoyed) My homework!
What does it look like?

Johnny: Can I help? (He proceeds to take a marker to her notebook and starts scribbling in it.)

Susie: (Now very upset) Hey! Stop it!
Go away! MOM!

At this point, Mom comes in and starts yelling at everyone. Now they are all miserable because no one had a good ending to this scenario.

Let's try it again, using successful confrontation. Susie and Mom have both discussed what successful confrontation looks like and how to use it. A while later (maybe even a couple of days later), this scenario takes place. Susie is again doing her homework at the dining room table, and in comes Johnny.

Johnny: Whatcha doin'?

Susie: My homework. (She notices Johnny's hand going for the marker.) Right now

I need to study. Here is a marker and
some paper. I need for you to sit over
there with it (points to chair opposite
of her) and make some pictures.
When I'm done we can draw together.
How does that sound to you?

At this point Johnny will either say, "OK" or "I don't want to" and proceed to go do something else. Either way it is a win-win solution.

As I said earlier, this technique can be used by anyone, anywhere, anytime—with coworkers, with friends, with family, and even in the classroom. I remember discussing the approach with a coworker, and he shared with me a true story. After demonstrating the technique to a six-year-old and using some positive reinforcement to encourage its use, he overheard a confrontation between the six-year-old and a neighbor child. The neighbor child was after the six-year-old's toy car. "I'm playin' with the car right now, but you can play with my truck, and when I get done we can do the car together. OK? Here . . ." stated the six-year-old, in a rather matter-of-fact way, as he handed over the truck. The neighbor child took the truck and played with it, giving no further thought to the car.

Something that should be handled early after diagnosis is explaining AD/HD to the siblings of the child. That way there are no secrets being kept or any shame being created about this disorder. Don't con yourself into thinking that siblings haven't experienced firsthand the child's behavior and its effects or your response to his behaviors. They know perfectly well something is going on. I might caution you again about going to the other end of the spectrum into overprotection. This is when you make AD/HD into such a big deal that everyone feels like they have to walk on eggs around the child. You'll know you're doing this if you hear things like this being said in your house: "Mom, he hit me again!" "Oh, Sally, you know it's just 'cause of his AD/HD. You'll just have to make do with it." Maybe the child did strike out because he wasn't focusing, but, if you've clearly defined the no-hitting rule, his behavior is not excused; he is still responsible for its effects.

TEAMWORK

Explain to the child's siblings in terms that they can comprehend what AD/HD is and that part of the treatment for this disorder means working together as a team. You're all on the same team, working toward the same end result—to create a more peaceful family life. Successfully living together takes teamwork, and everyone needs to contribute to the effort in order for the team to operate at its best. Explain that team members support one another. Help them realize that each person brings unique qualities to this team. Ask which qualities they are going to bring that will support the team's efforts and which ones they're willing to leave behind that may interfere with their effectiveness as team players. In turn, tell them what you're going to bring and leave behind. Impress upon them that without their input the team won't be as effective at working together toward its goal.

If someone in the family chooses not to be on the team, that's OK. It's her choice. Let her know, though, that you can't be responsible for her happiness in the family unless she is willing to take responsibility for herself by voicing her thoughts and feelings as a team member. Let her know she is welcome to join the team at any time and that you accept her decision no matter what.

In working out who brings what to the team, parents need to take into account the age and temperament of each family member. In other words, for Sally, who is a younger child and has a somewhat intense temperament, being a team member might mean using a calm tone of voice when telling her brother with AD/HD not to touch her toys instead of yelling at him. Or for Dan, an adolescent with a more tolerant, easygoing temperament, being a team member might entail assisting his brother on a project or assignment in order to help him stay focused. Observation will help you understand your family's dynamics, and then you can develop realistic strategies for working together as a team.

Family meetings are a fantastic tool to keep the team in good working order. All successful businesses rely on departmental meetings or board meetings to keep the company going. It's how everyone knows what everyone else is doing. Families are a lot like businesses, especially the family of today. Parents are truly domestic engineers—they do the work of the secretary, accountant, chef, maid, chauffeur . . . you get the idea. In order to keep things running smoothly in a family, you almost have to look at it like it's a business, and that's one reason for utilizing family meetings. Here's another. Various sources have reported that the average child over ten years of age (in a two-parent home) has only fourteen and a half minutes of interaction with his parents in twenty-four hours. Parents spend twelve minutes of this time issuing warnings or correcting things that have gone wrong, leaving only about two minutes per day or twelve to fourteen minutes per week of individual communication time, including collaborative activities, even working together. This is another good reason to have a family meeting. Basically, it's a time for the family to get together, usually once a week, and talk about what's going on in its various realms, make plans, handle scheduling, share concerns, brainstorm, come to agreements, and have some fun together. It's also a way of bringing things out into the open so that everyone feels like he has some input on how things are handled within the family.

What exactly goes on at these meetings? That's up to you and your family. You can have a very highly structured meeting, much like a business meeting, that would include a rundown of the previous week, minutes from the last meeting, upcoming scheduling, delegation of chores, discussion of current issues within the family, brainstorming to resolve those issues, and voting on resolutions. Or you could have an informal meeting that would include the basic concepts of a formal meeting, just not as highly structured. You will know, based on the dynamics of your family, which will work best for you. With either type, you should probably keep some kind of record of the meeting and any agreements made, perhaps in journal form. That way, if Susie says, "No, I never said I'd do that chore," you can look it up with her in the journal. A word of warning though—it goes both ways. Susie can also refer to the written record and say, "See, Mom. You did say that we were going to go to a movie on Tuesday night." When issues come up during the week, they can often be "tabled" until the next meeting, when thoughts, feelings, and ideas can be voiced in a safe atmosphere without the threat of any repercussions.

It's very important for parents not to play the role of overlord at these meetings. If this is the role you take, it will not be a safe atmosphere. You will only be giving the message to your children that their thoughts do not count and that, no matter what, the parents always win. Your relationship with your child will become a power struggle, and in ten years you'll be saying to yourself, "Why didn't he let me know he was having problems?" Why? Because it was never a safe thing to do. So change that now. It doesn't mean that the children become the overlords of the meeting either. This is what negotiation is for. The meeting should be a safe place with respect given to everyone's thoughts and feelings. By maintaining a safe environment for communication, you can prevent misbehavior from occurring and continue to build the relationships in your family that make for a more peaceful life.

If you've already made family meetings part of your home life, it's a good idea to review and update house rules every now and then. If you're just starting with family meetings, use the first couple of meetings to discuss and come to agreement on what the house rules should be and how they should be enforced. You'll definitely want to record this in the journal. It's a good idea to go over boundaries with everyone so that it's very clear where things and people should or should not be. For example, one of the boundaries I have clearly established with my own children is that my bathroom is just for me and that they are to use their own bathroom. Our home is small enough that it's not a big deal for them to walk thirty more feet and use the other bathroom. What is a big deal to me, though, is someone else leaving messes (toys, books, clothing) in my bathroom. If they want to make a mess, they need to do it in their own bathroom.

Having this rule and establishing this boundary is one way of being proactive. Now I don't have to get ticked off about stuff being left where it's not supposed to be—and I'm not yelling at my kids. I still have to intervene on occasion, but since the rules have been clearly established, I let them do the work for me and proactively reinforce them. Remember, we're talking about kids with AD/HD here, whose thoughts are going in ten different directions. Another example of proactive reinforcement might go like this: Johnny's walking out of the kitchen with a bowl of cereal. "Johnny, where should you be with that?" says Mom, pointing to the cereal. Johnny looks at Mom, "Huh? Oh . . . I need to be in the kitchen." "Thanks for remembering that rule," Mom replies.

It's a good idea to end your family meetings on a positive note; have some fun! Play a game, go on an outing, look at some old family pictures, or even bake or cook something together—whatever your family likes to do. This may be a huge stretch for you and your family if you're in the trenches of frustration. You may be saying to yourself, "Fun? What's that?" If so, all the more reason to do it. It's an opportunity to get to know one another all over again without the veil of frustration to keep you from seeing how wonderful everybody is. So many times we get blinded by this veil and can see only the negative; we actually forget what the positive looks like. You can even take turns each week and share in an interest of each family member. If your three-year-old likes to color, it will be a lot of fun—and quite interesting—for all to sit and color for a while. If your teenager likes rap music, it could be a lot of fun, and again quite interesting, to experience some rap music—as long as it's not too loud!

The message here is to lighten up and do so in a loving way. It goes back to changing our mind-sets. So many times we focus on the negative aspects of parenting, whether our child has AD/HD or not. We become so used to doing this that it can be very challenging to see the bright spots in life. Sometimes we forget that being a parent doesn't just mean being firm in order to mold and shape our children's futures; it also means being loving, for this also molds and shapes our children's destiny.

Chapter 4

Home Sweet Home: The Value of Organization

ow it's time to talk about that nasty word—organization. Don't let it scare you. Organization is really quite simple, and it is the key to a more peaceful home life for your family. Children with AD/HD and their families function much better in a highly structured, organized environment. That doesn't mean it has to be rigid or inflexible, just consistent. A consistent environment helps to decrease the misbehavior of the child and the stresses of the family. In chapter 2, I talked about observation. This is the first step in organizing and structuring the environment. As an observer you can sit back and see what triggers your child's episodes of misbehavior. Observing should be like watching a documentary and taking notes on its important elements. It will help you come up with a plan that you will implement gradually. This plan should be about how you can structure to prevent misbehavior, what supervision and support are needed, and when that support would be most helpful.

SETTING GOALS

In developing your plan you will need to set goals. Your first concern when setting goals is readiness. Is your child ready to work toward the goal? Are you ready to guide him? Are you both up to the physical, emotional, and mental challenges? What about your time schedules? Do you have to put in extra hours this week? Does he? If so, maybe this should wait another week. Be flexible with your plans as circumstances change. During busy times of your life and his, focus on very short lessons; during vacation or relaxed times teach more complex skills. This will keep the frustration level low for you and your child. A goal is much more attainable when the child knows what's expected, has the necessary equipment, and understands what the end result should be.

Make sure that the goals you set are short range, for both yourself and the child. The reason for this is that pursuing a single long-term goal means long-term frustration, but combining five short-term goals to achieve that one long-term goal eliminates much of that frustration. It's like the saying "Just for today." If you take on a task and know that all you have to do is handle that task just for today, you will be much more successful at completing it, whereas if you take on that same task and know that it's going to take a year to complete, you won't be as motivated, and your chances of success are less.

Live by the rule of doing only one thing at a time. Don't go on to another task until you've completed what you are working with. In this way your child is involved in only one activity at a time. You can always tell when you haven't enforced this rule with your child. You walk into the living room after an hour or so, and you literally can't see the floor. Toys are everywhere. Or with older kids, it's their bedroom floors that disappear. You go in to help them pick up, and every time you touch something, you get the response, "Wait, I'm using that right now." And you think to yourself, "How can she be using all the things in this room at the same time?" Remember? She's got AD/HD—she has the ability to do this! Life is much simpler, then, if you live by the rule "Do one thing only, and do it well."

You need to define the boundaries of an action or task. Soon he'll realize, "I can start playing on the computer when I've put all of the pieces of my model car kit away." Don't let the child cross over the boundary line of task one and just jump into task two. First he has to complete task one. Completing a task may be something as simple as putting things away. If the child is playing with a game, the game isn't complete until it's put back where he found it. Try to keep him playing with, working with, or being involved with only one thing at a time.

If you are wondering why I am stressing this so emphatically, it's for this simple reason: You need to get this basic rule down pat now and teach your child that he doesn't go to step two until he completes step one. Each step progressively builds upon itself. If your child doesn't learn this now, when he is eighteen or twenty years old, he'll be asking himself, "Gosh, what should I do now? Should I get married? Should I get a job? Or should I go to college? I don't know how to decide. What should I do first?" He didn't learn how to build progressively upon each step back at the beginning.

STRUCTURE

By the time your kids reach the age of eighteen, they will have spent over thirty thousand hours under your guidance and training. It takes around two thousand hours of classroom and outside study time to complete a bachelor's degree and half that to learn a vocational skills trade. This means your home has sixteen times more teaching time than a university. What do you want to do with that time? You are the most influential teacher your child will ever have, and your home is the most important school your child will ever attend. Structuring the home life and environment of a child with AD/HD enables her to have the education she needs to cope in life.

Structure can come from routine, a type of internal structure. The child knows what to expect at a certain time every day. Examples of this are after-school routines and bedtime routines. There are also various forms of external structure that you can implement in your home—for example, rearranging a play area or bedroom. Both internal and external structure provide order to compensate for the internal chaos the child with AD/HD experiences. I might mention here, too, that the idea of implementing routines and structure is how many successful adults with AD/HD have coped with and compensated for their disorder. They have learned to use this tool to their advantage in both their home lives and their professional lives.

Structuring means carefully placing and arranging objects and activities ahead of time and following an orderly process and routine in order to prevent problems from occurring. It's a way of being proactive rather than reactive. A lot of thought needs to go into structuring an environment. Once you know what it is that needs to be changed, make the changes gradually. Nothing is more unsettling to a child with AD/HD than a completely transformed world. If you think you saw hyperactivity before, wait until you see the child try to investigate every change that was made. It is much easier to field questions on one or two particular changes than to answer thousands of questions on every aspect of a new environment.

There is no end to the things you can change to simplify your life and the life of your child. A problem many parents face is that they try to change too much too soon. This is only natural; you want to get out of the insanity and into a more peaceful family life. This can happen only if you take it slow. Remember, taking one step at a time is just as important for you as it is for your child.

Create Environmental Boundaries

Cut back on the number of toys and create play centers in each room. Leave out a few toys in a box or basket in each room and put the rest away. Be ready to rotate toys, depending on your child (you'll know when to do this). By creating play centers you make each room user-friendly. For example, you might have an art center in the kitchen, a game center in the dining room, manipulatives in the living room, water toys in the bathroom, and so forth.

You can use this same procedure with books—leave out a few and rotate the rest.

Besides stating what belongs in a specific room and what doesn't, you will need to define where, exactly, in that room items can be worked with. For example, if your child likes to build model airplanes, that's going to mean working with small pieces, glue, and paint. Sounds like a project for the kitchen table to me. But I personally don't want paint marks left on my table. So what do I do? I define the exact work area by having the child do this work not only at the table, but also on a sheet of newspaper, a placemat, or even an old cutting board. The work must stay on this, within this area on the table. If it doesn't, that tells me he's not working with it respectfully and needs to put it away: "Johnny, you'll need to put this away now, and you can try it again tomorrow (or later). Thanks." As I'm saying this, I may need to guide him in the process of putting things away. I don't need to engage verbally any more than this. If I do, it may become a power struggle.

Another trick I picked up while teaching is to use small area rugs to accomplish the same thing. If a child has something to work with or play with on the floor, teach her that it must be kept on the rug. You can have a couple of extra area rugs rolled up in the corner of the room. And before she can get the toys out, she first has to put a rug down to work on. When she's done playing, she also has to roll the rug back up before the activity is considered put away.

You can even use that wonderful tool, duct tape, for defining environmental boundaries. One of the things I can remember from childhood is my parents saying, "Get back away from that TV—you're too close!" Of course, like all kids, I thought, "I'll never say stuff like that to my kids." Guess what? I did. We all do, actually. And then we realize, "Oh, no, I've become my parents!" But sometimes that's not all bad, as in this case of TV watching. After I heard myself say that, I came up with an idea to be more proactive about it. The next morning when my children went to turn on the TV, they noticed a piece of duct tape across the floor in front of it. "Mom, what's this for?" they asked. "I'm glad you noticed that!" I responded. "I feel like I'm always nagging you about how close to sit to the TV. So, instead, I put some tape down. You need to sit behind the tape to watch TV. If you choose not to, the TV will get turned off." No more TV problem. I didn't have to nag anymore because the duct tape did the work for me. It only took a month or two before we no longer needed to use the duct tape.

Put Things at Child Level

Instead of yelling at your kids for climbing on top of the refrigerator to get some crackers, make a snack center for them. Give them space in a drawer or part of a cupboard. Put in things like plastic dishes, cups, utensils, prepackaged snacks, and cereal. Give them space in the refrigerator for a small pitcher of water, juice, or milk, and fresh fruits and vegetables. As with any of these suggestions, set limits and be ready to guide them through the steps. This might sound like an open invitation for a really messy situation, and it could be if it is not presented in a simple, thorough manner. You have to be willing to guide them through the process of how to pour a glass of milk and clean up afterwards and be consistent with it—otherwise be ready for some more stress. Yes, they can clean up after themselves. They are capable of this but may need to be shown how. They should have access to a sponge, towel, dustpan, and broom.

The rule of putting things at their level holds true for every room, including the bathroom. Put towel hooks at their level (I suggest the use of hooks over towel bars, as they can't be used to swing on). Put whatever they may need in a place accessible to them so they won't need to climb on the fixtures. This doesn't mean putting your good china in an easy-to-reach place. If they shouldn't be touching it, it should be locked away out of sight. As we all know, for children with AD/HD, out of sight doesn't necessarily mean out of mind. That's why it needs to be locked in a way that they cannot unlock it.

Organize the Bedroom

Treat bedrooms as a child's or parent's private world, with admission by invitation only. Anything a child doesn't want others to play with should be placed in the play center in his room. The bedroom of a child with AD/HD needs to be structured, just like any other room. Hooks can be hung for clothes, pj's, and so forth. Dressers and closets full of clothes can be overwhelming for your child. Choosing an outfit for the day can be a stressful situation for both parent and child. By placing only a few outfits in the closet and a few articles of clothing in the dresser you can eliminate this stressor. In some cases it is even a good idea to eliminate the dresser and use bins instead. It's also helpful to have the entire outfit, socks and all, on one hanger so that the child doesn't have to search for matching pants, socks, and so on. One more tip: Don't tell him to make his bed until you have shown him how to do it; it doesn't need to be perfect and, again, any attempt should be acknowledged.

Any environment can be restructured to meet the needs of children with AD/HD and their families. The house, the yard, and the car can all be structured to meet everyone's needs. A key point to remember is to keep the environment as simple as possible: The more external stimuli in the environment, the greater the distractibility factor. When you decrease the clutter, you increase your child's ability to focus.

ROUTINES

Parents need to establish routines for highly stressful times of the day. These times could be before school, at mealtimes, after school, homework time, chore time, or bedtime. You will know when to implement a routine by, once again, using the tool of observation. If you've kept an observation journal you may notice a pattern of misbehavior at the same time every day. This is a good indicator of the need to implement a routine. The process involves seeing what's going on at the time of the problem behavior and then proactively brainstorming about what you can do to eliminate the triggers for the problem behavior.

You should work at routines gradually. Start out with one specific behavior: Make note of it and what's going on at the time it occurs, decide on a "positive" to replace the "negative," and then break the learning process up into small steps. What you don't want to do is to chart every waking minute of the day. Eventually you will have a pretty good idea of what a routine day looks like, but at this stage of the game, to keep from overwhelming yourself and your child, take it one step at a time.

For example, suppose mornings are a really difficult time for your child. You might even say they are chaotic. Think of how you might want the child's mornings to look. What will make them more positive? The first stressor could be that as soon as your child gets up she's watching TV. This creates problems later when it's time to get dressed, eat breakfast, and get out the door for school. Replacing this established negative routine with a positive routine might involve making a new rule that she doesn't watch TV until she has dressed herself, eaten breakfast, and gotten her things ready for school. It's also a good idea to put a time limit on the amount of TV watched, with the ideal being to eliminate it altogether, in the morning at least. Your first step is to explain this routine clearly to her several times the night before. It might sound like this:

> Susie, I've noticed mornings are a little hectic for us, and I'd like for us to make that different. Would you be willing to help me do that? . . . OK, here's what it's going to look like. When we wake up in

the morning the first thing we need to do is get
dressed. Next, we need to wash up, and then
we'll eat breakfast. When everything for school is
ready to go, we'll turn on TV for ten minutes. How
does that sound? ... Good. Now, so we're both
clear about this, tell me what you heard me say.....
Great! I can hardly wait for tomorrow morning!

Then during dinner, ask your child to share the special, new routine
with the family. This reconfirms it for her. And then, at bedtime,
make it into a quick, exciting list: "Remember, Susie, tomorrow's
our special, new morning routine. First we get dressed, then wash
up, then eat, then watch TV."

Here's another example: Suppose when Johnny gets home from
school he always fights with me about starting his homework. I've
also noticed that I'm asking him to do this as soon as he gets in
the door at 3:00. We start arguing back and forth, then he throws
his books down, runs to his room, and slams the door. Every day
it's the same thing. There are a lot of aspects of this scenario that
I can change in order to be proactive rather than reactive—for
instance, creating a supportive welcome-home ritual to take the
place of arguing. I take note of those things, write them down,
and incorporate them into a new routine. As I'm doing this, I'm
including the child in the process, letting him know what's going
on and getting his input. That might sound like this: "So, Johnny,
I've noticed that you and I have been arguing a lot about your
homework. I don't want to argue with you, and I know you don't
like it either. I've come up with a few ideas that might help, and
I'd like to hear your ideas about it, too." Johnny and I share our
ideas, negotiating and compromising. "Would you like to start your
homework at 3:30 or at 4:00?" And so on, until agreement is
reached about what the homework routine will look like and
when it will start. I casually remind him about the new homework
routine frequently until the day and the time it actually starts.

"Hey, Johnny. Welcome home. Do you remember what we agreed to start today? . . . Yep, that's right—you have 'till 4:00. Thanks!"

Consistency is the key to routines. The more consistent you are with them, the more success you will have. If a change in routine is necessary, explain to your child why and be ready to go through the changes step by step. If you are inconsistent, don't expect your child to be consistent. The principle of consistency means helping the child know what's expected, what the task is, what the process involves, and that wrong choices result in logical or natural consequences (more about this in chapter 7). Consistency is NOT sameness. It doesn't mean constructing minute-by-minute routines, nor does it mean that the child always puts everything away—that's perfection (and also insane). Consistency is reinforced with orderliness—but also with fun!

The morning routine discussed earlier is an example of one that gives the family a standard around which other activities can be established—in other words, breakfast. A simple routine or schedule should give a sense of consistency by establishing times to do certain things like dressing, eating, playing, doing chores or homework, and so on. The idea is to teach your child to handle the basics efficiently so that he has a foundation to build on. Keep the schedule adaptable but solid enough to give a basic structure to life. A simple routine is like putting gelatin powder into water: After setting, it holds the liquid in a form that doesn't run all over.

CHARTS

After you establish a few routines during the day, you can incorporate the use of charts. Again, it's important to take things slowly. It's not a good idea all of a sudden to have the child's entire day scheduled out and to place ten brand-new, color-coded, graphically designed charts in front of her and say, "These will help you!" This will put you both on a one-way course to failure. Take it one step at a time!

Charts give constant visual reminders and, even better, they are silent! No more yelling and nagging—at least not as much. They serve as great reminders for everyone. All you need to do is get some posterboard and either write out or draw pictures (depending on the age of your child) of the steps she's supposed to follow. Try to keep charts plain, yet interesting and attractive.

There are various types of charts you can use: chore charts, goal charts, daily charts, routine charts, and so on. A good one to start with is a routine chart. It can be hung in the child's bedroom, describing her morning routine or any routine that you are currently working on. Eventually you'll want to incorporate more than one routine into the day, but not on the same chart. For examples, refer to the following homework and bedtime charts.

Another type of chart, the chore chart, lists everyone's household chores for the day or the week. It should be displayed in a central location, like the kitchen. It's important that you include your and your partner's names along with the children's on this chart. A system that I've found works very well is a lottery. This chore chart consists of a piece of posterboard with an envelope for each family member taped to it. Each chore is written down on a card with a description of how to complete it. The cards are then placed faced down on a table and everyone takes turns drawing an equal number. After all the cards are drawn each person can then either keep the cards they have or negotiate with another family member to trade cards. The cards are then placed in each person's envelope on the chore chart. Now everyone has chores for the week. A variation of this is to make up two different types of cards, one set for daily chores and one for weekly chores. On the top of each card you can identify the chore as either daily or weekly. Please take a look at the sample chore chart on page 94.

A calendar chart like the sample on page 95 shows a month's worth of activities in a large calendar format. It also needs to be put in a centrally located spot. On it put everyone's appointments, project due dates, meetings, extracurricular activities, trips, visits—

SAMPLE HOMEWORK CHART

2:45 Welcome home!

- Put shoes and book-bag in bin.

- Hang up coat.

- Change clothes and hang up uniform.

3:00 Free time

- Have a snack.

- Play with toys or play outside or watch TV.

3:45 Pick up

- Put away toys, books, etc.

4:00 Homework

- Give Mom any notes from school.

- Do your assignments.

4:30 Finish up.

- When homework is done, have Mom check it.

- Put books and papers back in book-bag.

- Put book-bag back in bin.

- Go and play!

---

anything you can think of that a member of your family has to do. This enables you to support one another in your endeavors. Planning for this chart can be handled at the family meeting. Each person may prefer to have an individual calendar chart. Personally, I find using a day planner helps for this. For someone with AD/HD, though, a chart that is always in the same spot may be more helpful. These calendar charts can be reviewed on a weekly basis at the family meeting.

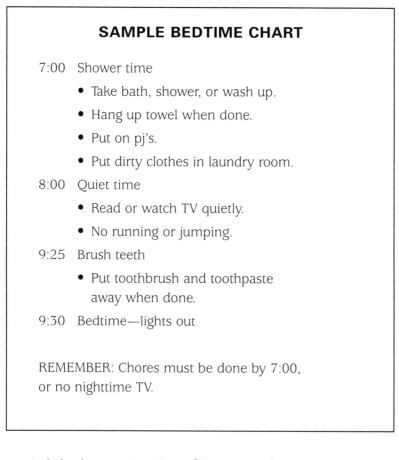

SAMPLE BEDTIME CHART

7:00 Shower time

- Take bath, shower, or wash up.
- Hang up towel when done.
- Put on pj's.
- Put dirty clothes in laundry room.

8:00 Quiet time

- Read or watch TV quietly.
- No running or jumping.

9:25 Brush teeth

- Put toothbrush and toothpaste away when done.

9:30 Bedtime—lights out

REMEMBER: Chores must be done by 7:00, or no nighttime TV.

A daily chart is an outline of the events that normally happen in your child's day. You can decide with him what the important activities are in a typical day and, if you want, allot a certain amount of time for each. A daily chart like the sample given on page 96 can be used in combination with the other charts or alone instead of routine charts, once the child has the routines down pat.

A schedule or routine is reassuring to a child because of its predictability. If your home is orderly, the child is less likely to be overwhelmed and frustrated. Any deviation from the routine, whether it is rearranging the furniture or a sudden trip to the store, needs to be announced ahead of time. If the change happens

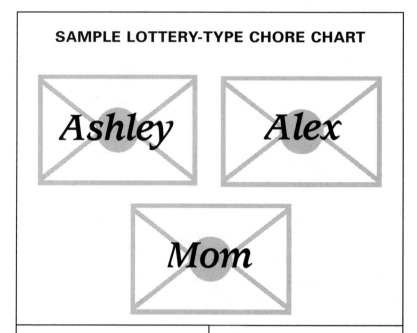

SAMPLE LOTTERY-TYPE CHORE CHART

Ashley

Alex

Mom

Ⓓ

Organize bookshelf and video cabinet.

1. Straighten books on shelf, making sure no books are on floor.

2. Put all videos back in cabinet.

3. Straighten videos in cabinet and close doors on cabinet.

*Example of daily chore card. D in corner stands for daily.

Ⓦ

Take out garbage.

1. Empty garbage cans from both bathrooms and family room into kitchen garbage.

2. Ask Mom to help you empty kitchen garbage and carry out to cans.

3. Put new trash bags into all garbage cans.

4. On Thursday night, take garbage cans out to curb.

*Example of weekly chore card. W in corner stands for weekly.

			SAMPLE CALENDAR CHART			
			September			

Sun	Mon	Tu	Wed	Th	Fri	Sat
					1 Alex dentist 4:15	**2** Library trip
3 Church 11:00 Picnic in the park	**4** Ashley gymnastics 4:00	**5** Visit Daddy 5:00	**6**	**7** Alex brings snacks for school	**8** Ashley spelling test	**9** Mom's day out
10 Grocery Shopping after church	**11** Ashley gymnastics 4:00	**12** Visit Daddy 5:00	**13**	**14** 1/2 day	**15** Ashley spelling test	**16** Library trip
17 Church	**18** Ashley gymnastics 4:00	**19** Visit Daddy 5:00	**20**	**21**	**22** Ashley spelling test	**23** Mom's day out
24 Church Grocery shopping after church	**25** Ashley gymnastics 4:00	**26** Visit Daddy 5:00	**27**	**28** Alex brings snacks for school	**29** Ashley spelling test	**30** Library trip

---

SAMPLE DAILY CHART

7:00	Get up; take medicine
7:00–7:15	Get dressed (upstairs); brush teeth
7:15–7:30	Eat breakfast
7:30	Make sure things are ready to go by front door
7:30–7:45	TV time
7:45	Leave for school
8:00–3:30	School
3:30	Come home
3:30–4:00	Homework
4:00–5:00	Free play
5:00–5:30	Pick up room
5:30–6:00	Dinner
6:00–6:30	TV time
6:30–7:30	Free play/computer time
7:30–8:00	Bath, brush teeth
8:00–8:30	Quiet time
8:30	Bedtime

---

suddenly, be prepared to give the child extra help. Also, avoid sudden endings to activities. A five-minute countdown is really helpful to signify the upcoming change of activity; using a timer is another good method.

Goal charts can be used to change a specific behavior. When, from your observations, you have seen a pattern of ineffective behavior, you can choose to replace it with a more effective pattern. This effective pattern would be the goal. You can use a reward system to achieve that goal. Rewards and reinforcements will be discussed in chapter 7. For now, though, you may notice when looking at the sample goal chart that the rewards—make popcorn; take a trip to the park—are not of a material nature. In other words, we are not "buying" good behavior with money or merchandise. The sample on the next page shows a chart for keeping a neat bedroom.

The charts you see in this chapter are ones designed for this text. The charts I actually use in my home are basically just words and pictures drawn on posterboard and designed in part by my children. I draw the pictures and they color them in, or I write the words and they trace them. The charts don't need to be complex in order to be effective. Keep them simple. The more complex they are, the harder they will be for you to reinforce and for the child to follow through on.

SAMPLE GOAL CHART

Goal

Bedroom is neat. This means bed is made and all clothes, toys, and books are put in their proper places. Check at 7:30 A.M. (2 points). Check at 6:00 P.M. (2 points).

Points Earned

	SU	M	TU	W	TH	F	SA
First Week	0	//	0	//	////	//	////
Second Week	0	////	////	//	//	////	////
Third Week							
Fourth Week							

Possible Rewards

Play Monopoly Jr. with Mom	12
Soft drink from refrigerator	4
Make popcorn	4
Trip to the park	24
Stay up till 9:00 on school night	16
Bike ride with Mom downtown	24

Chapter 5

What Do We Do Now? A Look at Diagnosis and Treatment

*T*hough there is no cure for AD/HD, there are a great many ways to cope and compensate, ways of "retraining the brain" that can be of great benefit to both the child and her family. But before you can begin to work with this disorder and develop a treatment plan, the child must undergo a thorough diagnostic procedure so you know just what you are dealing with.

DIAGNOSIS: A COMPLICATED PUZZLE

Diagnosing AD/HD is a complicated process, much like putting together a puzzle. An accurate diagnosis requires an assessment conducted by a well-trained professional such as a developmental pediatrician, a child psychologist or psychiatrist, or a pediatric neurologist. These professionals should be familiar with AD/HD and all of the other disorders that have symptoms similar to those of AD/HD. These other disorders are known as "imitator disorders," and there are a multitude of them, including the following:

- Anxiety disorders, mood disorders, dissociative disorders, personality disorders, depression, learning disorders (such as central auditory processing disorders), profound conditions (autism), distorted reports of misbehavior, appeals for attention, conduct disorders, developmental delays, and extreme emotional disturbances

- Personality changes due to general medical conditions, such as hearing and visual perception problems, iron deficiency, lead intoxication, neurological disorders (i.e., encephalitis, fracture, tumor, etc.), malnutrition, diabetes, hypoglycemia, thyroid disorders, and sleep disorders

- Food allergies

- Substance abuse–related disorders

- Psychosocial stressors such as parental abuse, divorce, death of a loved one, or disasters (these can result in temporary symptoms of inattention, impulsivity, and overactivity that generally arise suddenly and have no long-term history)

AD/HD is not diagnosed if the symptoms are better accounted for by another one of these disorders. In all of them, the symptoms of inattention are present but have an onset after the child is seven, and the child's history of school adjustment is generally not characterized by disruptive behaviors or teacher complaints. The diagnostician needs to rule out all of these imitator disorders because they will not be helped by the same treatments one would use for AD/HD. If the diagnostician is not well trained in these areas, it's best to seek a different referral.

A comprehensive assessment of your child should begin with a complete physical, followed by:

- A detailed medical and family history obtained in interviews with the parents, the child, and the child's teachers

- Behavior rating scales completed by parents and teachers

- Observation of the child

- Diagnostic testing, including academic assessments; testing for learning disabilities; tests for language and reading skills; personality trait analyses; screening checklists;

tests for social and emotional functioning and developmental abilities; and measures of attention span, impulsivity, and intelligence

To eliminate other disorders, the diagnostician will get medical histories and behavioral backgrounds for both the parents and the child. More than likely, the diagnostician will go over a list of AD/HD indicators with the parents. The AD/HD diagnosis is made on the basis of observable behavioral symptoms in multiple settings. This means that the person doing the evaluation must collect data from multiple sources. A single interview or rating scale of the child cannot replace the combined observations of parents, family members, teachers, and mental health professionals.

Children with AD/HD rarely show any visible signs of the disorder during visits to their physicians. They characteristically behave well in interview situations, particularly when they are one-on-one. Therefore, a well-trained diagnostician knows not to make a determination based solely upon how the child behaves when they are together. Sophisticated medical tests such as EEGs or MRIs are not part of the routine assessment. Such tests are usually only given when the diagnostician suspects another problem, and those cases are infrequent.

After completing the evaluation, the diagnostician makes one of three determinations: (1) the child has AD/HD; (2) the child doesn't have AD/HD but his difficulties are the result of another disorder or other factors; or (3) the child has AD/HD and a coexisting disorder. To figure out if the child has AD/HD, the diagnostician compares his or her findings to the criteria spelled out in the fourth edition of the American Psychiatric Association's *Diagnostic and Statistical Manual of Mental Disorders.* (For the complete criteria, please see the appendix of this book.) According to those criteria, the child's symptoms must be present before the age of seven, must be considered inappropriate for the child's age, and must "cause clinically significant impairment in social and academic functioning." In making a determination, the diagnostician must realize that AD/HD can and often does coexist with other disorders, particularly learning disabilities, oppositional defiant disorder, and conduct disorder. Clearly, the diagnosis is not as simple as reading a symptom list and saying, "This child has AD/HD."

TREATMENT OPTIONS

Soon after a diagnosis of AD/HD has been made, you will need to develop a treatment plan, or, in other words, answer the question "What do we do now?" To do this you need to educate yourself about the various treatment options. There are several to consider:

- Medication

- Behavior management training (parent training or counseling)

- Academic interventions, such as special education classes, a resource room, tutoring, or intervention by the teacher using behavior management in the classroom

- A combination of any or all of the above

You could also ignore the problem and pretend it will go away. But let me give you a hint—this last idea doesn't work. The best approach seems to be a multimodal approach—that is, a combination of treatments, such as combining behavior management and academic interventions; medication and behavior management; medication and academic interventions; or medication, behavior management, and academic interventions.

Not only does ignoring AD/HD not work, neither does using medication alone. You cannot just give a child medication and think that the AD/HD will take care of itself. Medication allows the child to get a grip on herself, not on her behavior. She can still choose to act ineffectively. The difference is that a child on medication can be taught to make effective choices, whereas a child who is not can't realize those options. If you do use medication, you must also employ behavior management at home or at school, or at both, to change behavior. Whatever approach you choose, whether it includes medication or not, it should be a multimodal approach. If you choose not to use medication, that's fine, but make sure you are using some sort of behavior management with the child both at home and at school. I'll say more about the medications used to treat AD/HD later in this chapter.

The previous list of treatment options identifies the only ones that I personally advocate. I am a firm believer that unless there are hard facts and data, controversial treatments should be avoided. On the other hand, every child is different—if you find something that works, go for it.

THE TREATMENT TEAM

When you follow up a diagnosis of AD/HD with treatment, you will need to create a treatment team. A team approach can provide you and your child with the best help available. So, who are these team members? The main members and some ways they work together are next described. You may need other helping professionals on your team, depending on your needs and the needs of your child, especially if overlapping conditions or disorders are involved.

Before I go on, let me clarify how important it is to allow other members of the treatment team to be valuable to you. There is a reason for this. In order for people to want to be part of the treatment team, you have to create a desire for them to be there. If you are constantly negating them by not allowing them to do their jobs or be who they are, they won't want to be part of your team. They won't be willing to give a 100 percent effort. They won't support you. In the case of a child with AD/HD, we need all the support we can get.

Supervisor(s)

The supervisor or cosupervisors are the parent or parents of the child—in other words, you. In this position you will serve as observer, moderator, public relations person, recording secretary, and, not least, chief communicator. You are responsible for keeping all the lines of communication open—in short, making sure the right hand knows what the left hand is doing. Your role requires you to be a good listener and observer. You will need to see and hear what's going on and what others have to say without letting your personal judgment cloud the issue. This rule also holds for another of your responsibilities: monitoring and evaluating the child's progress in relation to the treatment plan. You will also be in charge of the archives—all the records and documentation about your child and AD/HD. As supervisor you will also need to have an honest and open relationship with your child. You will need to create a safe environment and earn your child's trust. If you are unable to do this, the child may be unwilling to take part in the treatment plan.

The parent's role as supervisor involves quite a bit, but don't be overwhelmed—that won't help anyone. It's not a "job" or "chore." It's an adventure! Parents are an incredible source of information for everyone on the treatment team. You are the eyes and ears for the team, and your inside information is a valuable resource. It is important to be confident of your ability in this role. Stay informed and up to date about AD/HD; learn whatever is necessary so that you can find the best possible care and use the most effective treatment options. Build your knowledge by asking questions and searching until you find the answers. And speaking of questions, drop the fear of asking "stupid" questions, whether it's communicating with professionals or your next-door neighbor. There is no such thing as a stupid question. When you don't ask questions because of this fear, you are denying others the right to be valuable members of this team and your life.

Learn to trust your observations and judgments, for they are essential. Be supportive of other members of the treatment team. Be willing to accept information given to you before passing judgment on it. Be very clear as to what each team member expects of you so you may assist in facilitating the treatment plan. On the same note, it's important for you to remember that you don't have all the answers and you don't need to. Be honest, calm, and confident in your desire to help your child, but avoid the "I'm the parent, so I know what's best" attitude. Instead, remember this: "I know a lot, and I'm learning more!"

Captain

Your child is the captain of the treatment team. The child's role is even more important than your role as supervisor. His job is to be himself; he should feel free to express his thoughts and feelings (in an appropriate way) to any member of the team. His position is at the heart of the team. In order to be successful as a team member, he needs to be aware of his diagnosis and how it affects him and his life. He needs to be able to work with all the other team members and be aware of what their respective roles are with regard to the treatment plan.

Academic Advisor(s)

The academic advisor—or advisors, as the case may be—is your child's teacher, as well as academic support staff when appropriate. This role of academic advisor involves being an effective observer, educator, and evaluator. It also includes adapting or adjusting the child's curriculum, building self-esteem and social skills, and monitoring treatment with respect to education. Though the academic advisor's observations are important in making a diagnosis, the advisor is not a diagnostician, nor should she be expected to be.

Chapter 6 looks at the role of the academic advisor in more detail, especially the parent-teacher relationship.

Treatment Engineer

The treatment engineer is the child's doctor. Whether or not medication is part of the treatment, this role includes monitoring health care. If medication is chosen, the doctor can prescribe the correct one and the proper dosage. This role is also one of educator, in that the doctor needs to share all pertinent information with the respective team members. This includes sharing available resources and research.

You'll need to look for a doctor with whom you and your child can have a good working relationship. He needs to be skilled and knowledgeable about AD/HD, or at least willing to become more educated about it. He should earn your trust, be realistic and candid about the situation, and not instill false hopes. The doctor should be able to give you an outline of treatment procedures—what steps to take and when—and how these steps relate to the expected development of your child.

Some doctors are not confident when it comes to diagnosis and treatment of AD/HD. It's questionable how much accurate and consistent training is provided in residency programs, so doctors' uneasiness is understandable. The good news is that this trend is changing as greater numbers of doctors gain direct experience with the families of children who have AD/HD and, even better, take it upon themselves to become more educated in this area. The bad news is the amount of inconsistency in diagnosis and treatment of the disorder. Some doctors never prescribe medication; others always prescribe medication. Some go overboard on testing procedures; others go strictly by observation of the child in the office. Some in this last group make diagnostic decisions on the misleading basis of how the child behaves during a ten-minute office visit.

If you already have a good working relationship with your family doctor, you should be able to be honest with each other. If either one of you does not feel comfortable with the testing process, ask for a referral. If you have a doctor who is honest about her capabilities, she will more than likely suggest this before you even ask. At this stage she will probably refer you to a teaching hospital or specialist. They, in turn, will do the testing, rule out any imitator disorders, give an accurate diagnosis, and advise you on follow-up treatment. Then they will either send you back to your doctor to continue treatment or suggest a doctor who specializes in AD/HD.

All children need routine health care, whether or not they have AD/HD. When you have a child who is affected by a health condition, it's especially important to be consistent with health care. It always amazes me how vigilant some people are about caring for their automobiles, yet they can't remember the last time they went to their doctors. Our bodies need tune-ups just as much as our cars do. Whether or not you choose medication as a treatment option, your child needs routine health care. It's important to stick with one doctor rather than doing the doctor hop—a doctor for shots, a doctor for colds, a doctor for physicals, and so forth—unless, of course, specialists are required. Even then, it's a good idea to go to your regular doctor first so he's aware of the situation.

Proactively planning enhances communication with all team members, especially your child's doctor. It allows everyone to feel valuable. Be prepared. If it's your first visit with the doctor, be ready with teacher evaluations, medical histories and evaluations, a family history, parent evaluations, and a summary of any observed social skill problems. You should take along your own notes, journal of observations, any questions, and an up-to-date home/school rating scale.

Be sure to have your notes and questions in writing because once your child gets used to visiting the doctor, she will feel quite comfortable and "be herself"—in other words, somewhat distracting.

This method also enables you to jot down things at your leisure rather than trying to remember everything on the spot.

During any visit take notes, whether it's an initial consultation or a periodic checkup. You'll exchange valuable information, and in the same way that the doctor takes notes for your child's records, it's important for you also to take notes for your own records. Go in with the mind-set that you are both on the same team, rather than with the goal of conveying the message "Here's the proof—medicate him." That's not a healthy or successful attitude to have.

For a child with AD/HD, going to a doctor's appointment is a transition. Be prepared and build up to it. Call ahead to find out how long a wait you can expect before you actually see the doctor. Make the child aware of this and suggest she bring something to keep herself occupied. I know for myself that a visit to my children's doctor can be emotionally traumatic if I or my children are not prepared. When my children were younger, they had a tendency to be extremely hyperactive in the doctor's office, so it was very easy for me to become caught up in their behavior rather than trying to absorb what the doctor had to say.

The following scenario illustrates how ineffective planning compares to effective planning for this type of transition. During a routine health care visit, a parent and doctor attempt to communicate while encountering interference from the child. The parent has valid concerns to be addressed, and the doctor is willing to listen and respond to those concerns. Because the child keeps getting in the middle, I call this situation "Keep Away."

> Dad: I have some questions I need to ask you ...
>
> Johnny: (Interrupting) Dad, I'm hungry! (Child jumps in between the parent and doctor.)
>
> Dad: Just a minute, Johnny. Doctor, I was wondering about ... (Tries to move the

child aside, but it doesn't work. Instead, tries moving away from the child.)

Johnny: (Interrupting, now pulling on parent's arm) I'm hungry. I want to go. Where's my Game Boy?

Dad: (Quickly losing patience) What? Stop it! Can't you see I'm busy?

Doctor: (Trying to stay focused) What was that you wanted to ask me?

Johnny: (Waving Game Boy he had in his coat pocket, still moving all over) Found it! Hey, you got any batteries? Some double As?

Dad: (Patience now gone) Johnny, get that out of the doctor's face! Go sit down!

Doctor: (Anxious to get to the next patient) Why don't we talk about this another time? If it's urgent I can call you after my rounds.

Dad: (Now frustrated with the whole situation) Oh ... well, that would be ...

Johnny: (Jumping back in front of parent) Hey, Dad, can we go? I'm hungry!

Obviously the parent is annoyed with the situation, and the child has no clue why. The doctor more than likely feels frustrated because he can't be of more help. This is not an effective way to get our questions answered. When we are not proactive it hinders us from communicating our concerns to others, and we set ourselves and our children up for failure. Let's try this again, only with a little proactive planning added in.

Dad:	Johnny, tomorrow after school we will be going to the doctor's office. So, what will we be doing tomorrow after school?
Johnny:	Going to the doctor's office. What's for dinner?
Dad:	Right now we're talking about your doctor's appointment. Sometimes we have to wait for your appointment. I'm taking a book to read. What are you going to take?
Johnny:	Nothin'.
Dad:	Would you like to take your library book or your Game Boy?
Johnny:	My Game Boy. Can I have some money to rent a movie?
Dad:	Right now we're talking about your doctor appointment. What are we talking about?
Johnny:	My appointment.
Dad:	Thanks. What was it you're going to take with you?
Johnny:	My Game Boy.
Dad:	Oh, yes, that's right. When we get to your appointment what should you do?
Johnny:	I don't know.
Dad:	You should choose a place to sit and play with your Game Boy. What should you do?

Johnny: I should choose a spot to sit and play my Game Boy.

Dad: Thanks for hearing me. When I'm speaking with the doctor, what should you do?

Johnny: Not interrupt.

Dad: Great idea! And you can play with your Game Boy while I do that.

Johnny: OK, I will. Can I go outside?

Dad: When we're done talking about your appointment you may. One last question: If you need to interrupt our conversation tomorrow, how should you handle that?

Johnny: Umm, oh yeah, put my hand on your arm and wait.

Dad: Great! I'm so glad you remembered! Thanks for talking with me about this.

If I proactively make this kind of prearranged agreement, I set myself, and my child, up for success. It takes not even five minutes to do this. And I'll reinforce it again by following through the next day and having a very similar conversation. Mind you, this is not a guarantee that my child will be an angel in the doctor's office. But I have established a pattern for effective behavior that is very reinforceable. When the time comes and I am conversing with the doctor, or anyone for that matter, I simply need to reinforce with consistency and persistency. Say I get in there and my child starts being intrusive and interrupting. I say, "Excuse me for one minute, doctor. Alex (touching his arm), right now you need to sit down and play with your Game Boy. What should you do?" Alex responds, "But I got to ask you something." My response: "You'll need to remember how to do that," as I guide him back to his seat. "Thanks. Now, doctor, I was wondering..." Soon after, Alex remembers, gets up, touches my arm, and quietly waits. As soon as there is a pause in our conversation, I say, "Thanks for getting my attention in a nice way. What do you need?" If your child is an effective interrupter but seems to do it excessively, you can include in your prearrangement just how many times he may interrupt. Each time he does effectively interrupt, you can remind him what number he's on and how many times he has left.

When you are not proactive, you sabotage yourself and your child. When you don't communicate effectively with others you sabotage yourself and the other person. You are basically denying the other person the right to be valuable to you. I know that when the situation is reversed and I'm the one trying to communicate with someone who is constantly interrupting, I feel slighted and unneeded in the conversation. I'm sure you've had this happen to you also. This is not about feeling guilty about something you may have done or even currently do. It's about looking honestly at how you communicate and saying to yourself, "Does this work for me? How effective is it? Actually, it feels ineffective, and I want to change it to be more effective. What can I do differently?" Then you can proactively plan ahead.

Making ourselves valuable and at the same time allowing others to be valuable to us is important to effective communication. The following scenario gives an example of how ineffective communication looks, sounds, and feels. During a routine health care visit, the parent and doctor attempt to communicate. In this example, the interference is coming from the parent, but it could just as easily be reversed. The parent has some valid concerns, and the doctor is willing to listen and respond to those concerns—that is, if she gets a chance.

Doctor: Mrs. Jones, I'm glad you could make it
so that we could discuss Susie's tests...

Mrs. Jones: (Cutting the doctor short) You know, I
didn't think it would take so long to
get them back. Does it usually take
this long? I guess it's understandable,
though, because you did so many tests
and, boy, I bet that bill will be a high
one. It's just terrible the cost of tests
these days, and you know why that is?
I'll tell you, it's because of people having
unnecessary tests done, that's why,
and, you know, I can remember going
to the doctor when I was a kid and
having to take tests. Boy, I didn't like
that! (She only stops because taking a
breath is a necessity.)

Doctor: Yes! Well, the results are back and we
were correct in our assumption that
Susie does have AD/HD. Now what
that . . . (Oops, she gets cut off again!)

Mrs. Jones: Oh! I knew it! You know, I was reading
a book about that and it sounded just
like her so I guess I could have saved
myself some time by not having all
these tests done, and you're not going
to suggest she take Ritalin, are you,
because I read about that too and I
think it's no good because that's what
the article said, so it must be true, and
she shouldn't take that kind of medication, she should take the other kind,
that "dexa" stuff. (Another slight pause
for air)

Doctor: I see.

At this point, the doctor stops talking for a moment to gather her thoughts—though she'd like to say it, she keeps the thought "Well, what do you need me for?" to herself. It's likely she is now realizing how challenging this situation may be and wondering if she will really be able to help. Someone is clueless here, and it's not the child or doctor this time. It's the parent. The doctor feels frustrated, to say the least, because she's being denied the right to be of service. This is also not an effective way to get our concerns answered. When we are intrusive and all-knowing, we make ourselves unapproachable. No one wins here: not the parent, not the doctor, and especially not the child. Let's try this again, only with a little open-mindedness and patience.

Doctor:	Mrs. Jones, I'm glad you could make it so that we could discuss Susie's test results. And I apologize for the delay.
Mrs. Jones:	That's no problem. I'm glad that you have them.
Doctor:	Well, the results concur with our previous assumptions that Susie does have AD/HD.
Mrs. Jones:	I see. (Pausing and waiting for more information to be given)
Doctor:	I'm sure you have a lot of questions, and I'm more than willing to answer them. First, though, let me go over these results with you.
Mrs. Jones:	That would be good. Do you mind if I take some notes?
Doctor:	Not at all—as a matter of fact, I have some copies here for you. (She then proceeds to explain the results, while the parent takes some notes, occasionally

> stopping her only for clarification.) I
> know this is a lot to digest. What are
> some of your questions?

Mrs. Jones:　Right now they're about treatments.

In this last scenario, the parent conducted herself as if she wanted to know more. By accepting, understanding, not interrupting, taking notes, and asking structured questions, she was able to gain more information. This allowed the doctor to be valuable to her and supply her with the information she desired. Occasionally, interruptions are necessary. When we find ourselves getting lost in the information, we need to make the other person aware of this. In this way we are also allowing the other person to be valuable.

Family Moderator

The family moderator is the mental health professional or counselor. A family moderator can be very valuable because AD/HD affects every aspect of your family's, as well as your child's, existence. This professional assists in the maintenance of the family's emotional stability and unity. His job is one of helping to keep things on the emotional up-and-up.

The primary goals of the counselor, as far as being a team member, are to assist in diagnosis and to help maintain the family's emotional stability and unity. The earlier she is asked to join the treatment team, the better. The counselor's first task may be to take part in the diagnostic phase. If certified as a clinical psychologist or psychiatrist, she may even serve as the main diagnostician. By this I mean she would do the majority or all of the diagnostic testing and then turn the results over to the medical doctor. If this is the case, her part in this phase will usually require two or more interviews. Though the main purpose of these interviews is testing, the counselor will also obtain some other pertinent information by covering the following topics:

- Personal development

- Family relationships (parent-child, sibling, extended family)

- Activities outside the home

- Symptoms and indicators

- Parents' current knowledge of symptomatic behavior and techniques, if any, used to cope

- Support systems that are already established or may be needed

- Previous diagnostic and treatment attempts, if any

This type of information helps the counselor gain a clear picture of the psychological factors affecting both the child and family. It also clarifies which types of treatment would be most effective and what some possible issues may be for future counseling.

I find that some parents tend to be intimidated by the thought of seeing a counselor after the diagnostic phase has ended. These are usually the same parents who feel uncomfortable with the counselor's obtaining the previously mentioned information. They ask themselves, "What does my relationship with my child or husband have to do with my child's having AD/HD? Why do you need to ask that?" There's really no need to feel threatened by the counselor's attempts to obtain this information. As I said, the reason is to develop a treatment plan that is best going to meet your needs and the needs of your child. Seeing a counselor is not necessarily about having some huge traumatic issue to deal with—although this is how it's often been viewed in the past. You used to hear things like "Boy, you must be really messed up if you have to see a counselor!" Nowadays, most of us know better. You go to a counselor to help you find and maintain the balance in your life, and if anything major comes up, you'll be better equipped to handle it.

You might be saying, "That's all fine and good, but we've chosen medication, so we won't be needing a counselor." Wrong! Remember, the reality is that biochemical treatment only gets a grip on the child, not the behavior. The child may experience less hyperactivity while on medication, but the behavior problems are still there, just not as noticeable. Just because the child is medicated doesn't mean he's a saint. The difficulties that the child and family experience require the help of every team member. Generally, children with AD/HD who don't receive special assistance from other team members and who use only medication as a form of treatment do not succeed as well in school or in their relationships. Their overall emotional health and adjustment and their feelings of self-worth are compromised as well. That's why you need a counselor.

Just as it is important to develop effective communication with your child's doctor, it's equally important to do this with the counselor. It's common for people to withhold information. Fear is usually the motivator in these situations: "If he knew about that, he might think I'm bad or crazy." Wrong again. This time you're putting the counselor up on a pedestal. He's just someone whose job it is to serve as a listener and guide, to hear what's going on, and to steer you in a productive direction. By withholding information, you could be steering yourself in the wrong direction. The following interaction between counselor and parent makes this clear.

Counselor: So, how are things going?

Parent: (Shrugging shoulders, nodding head) Fine. (This is followed by a quick smile that switches automatically into a blank expression.)

Counselor: OK. (Thinks, "This is awkward.") So what's new? Anything going on you want to talk about? ("Maybe this will draw the parent into the conversation.")

Parent:	Nothing. (Purses lips and looks off to the side.)
Counselor:	(Thinks, "One of us might as well get to the point.") So, how's it going with Johnny?
Parent:	Fine. (Nodding head, still avoiding eye contact)
Counselor:	Oh, well, that's good. How's the observation journal coming along? What are some things you've noted in it? ("This will surely get a more detailed response!")
Parent:	(Thinking, "Darn, I got caught!") Well, I ... uhmm ... haven't really started it yet ... I ... I've just been so busy ... ("It's out of the bag now; I wonder what will happen now?")
Counselor:	(Thinking, "Yes! Verbalization at last.") Oh, well, you can start it this week. So, what's been keeping you so busy? Work, or family stuff?
Parent:	(Thinking, "Well, that wasn't so bad at all; I didn't get judged negatively for not starting that journal"; looking at counselor) Well, both, I guess. It's just a lot of things to do right now—kind of tiring. (Relaxing a little more now)
Counselor:	(Thinks, "Maybe this won't be so challenging and I can be of value.") Sounds like life is rather hectic for you right now. What are some things you're doing to take care of yourself?

And so the conversation goes. When we withhold information because of what we believe another's perceptions or judgments will be, we are cheating ourselves and shortchanging the other person. When we don't allow others to be valuable, we lose out on valuable information. The same holds true for constantly negating incoming information. When someone is continually contrary, it's like shutting a door in other people's faces. And when you get the door shut enough on you, you're not going to go back. The message comes across very clearly that "Your input is not valuable to me." In this last scenario, the parent realized that it was his own perception and judgment that was keeping him from effectively communicating and receiving valuable information.

MEDICATION

Now it's time to talk about that highly controversial subject: medication. Some people see medication as a blessing, others see it as a curse, and all are entitled to their opinions. What I will say about it is this: Do not pass judgment on it. Make an educated choice based on scientific fact and your knowledge of what's most beneficial to your child. Scientific facts are data that have been thoroughly researched. They are not biased news articles or uninformed opinions. Nor are they those little voices inside your head. You know the ones I mean: the ones that tell you, "Don't do that, or you're a bad parent." These voices should not be confused with your gut instincts. On the contrary, these voices come from the IBSC (Itty Bitty Shitty Committee). Remember, your gut instincts can be thought of as your wisdom guiding you; the IBSC is your subconscious getting in the way. There was a time when I let my IBSC guide me. It was not good. We were considering having our son tested for AD/HD and decided it would be a good idea to get some feedback from an unbiased third party, our family counselor. I say considering because, at the time, I was doubting myself, listening to my IBSC instead of my gut instincts.

All the telltale signs were there. His AD/HD differed from our daughter's, though, in that he was extremely aggressive and often displayed a violent temper. Even though our daughter had been diagnosed a few years before and we had been using medication as part of her treatment plan, we were leery of this step with our son. We were still in denial, not understanding how this could happen to us twice. Alex's father came right out and told the counselor that he did not like the idea of our son's having to take medication. Dennis, our counselor, replied, "You can't get a grip on Alex's behavior until you get a grip on Alex. What you're seeing when a child is medicated is what he would normally be like if he were not affected by this disorder. All the medication does is give him a chance for normalcy." We were shocked. Did he say normal? Our kids have a chance for normalcy? As an emotionally stable and deeply loving and committed parent, how could I deny my child the right to normalcy? I couldn't—not any more than the mother of a diabetic child could deny her child the right to normalcy.

The most productive attitude toward medication for AD/HD is to regard it as you would insulin for a child with diabetes or anti-seizure medication for a child with epilepsy. If you were told that your child had diabetes or epilepsy and had to take medication every day or risk severe symptoms, what would you do? Very few parents would respond, "I prefer to take a psychological approach to train my child not to have diabetes" or "That would be teaching my child to take the easy way out instead of taking responsibility for his illness." It's the same thing for a child with AD/HD.

I'm not saying that medication is the cure-all, only that in some cases it can be an asset in the treatment process. On the other hand, you can't give your child a pill and walk away thinking the medication will solve his behavior problems. Medication is a part— one part—of the treatment process. It is simply a filler for a chemical that isn't there, working to improve the symptomatic factors—in other words, the inattentiveness, impulsiveness, and so forth. It does not change behavior that is a result of ineffective choices. Again, just because a diabetic is on insulin, that doesn't mean he can eat anything he wants. He still has to follow a strict dietary regime. He has to modify his eating habits and behaviors. It's the same for a child with AD/HD. The medication allows the child to get a grip on himself and focus in the here and now. Once that's established you can begin working with the behaviors you want to change.

I remember working with a child both before and after his diagnosis of AD/HD. Before diagnosis, when he would hit another child I would explain to him, "We don't hit other people; if you're angry at someone you need to tell him how you feel." Of course, none of this registered with the child; he was already five steps down the line. After medication, however, we were able to establish a prestanding agreement about hitting; his brain now allowed him to comprehend the making of an agreement. When the situation called for me to remind him of the agreement, he was then able to get a grip on his behavior, express his feelings, and decide on what actions to take.

It's worth repeating that medication does not have to be a part of the treatment process; if it is, though, it should not be the only form of treatment. In chapter 1 I explained that the symptomatic behavior of AD/HD shows up in mild, moderate, and severe forms, and a child's symptoms can fall anywhere on that scale. So if your child is mildly affected by AD/HD there may not be a need for medication. Behavioral and educational interventions may suffice. More than likely, though, if your child is affected moderately to severely you will need to use medication in the treatment program.

Commonly Prescribed Medications

The most often prescribed medications for AD/HD are stimulants and antidepressants. Yes, stimulants. You have to remember that AD/HD is a chemical imbalance in the frontal lobe of the brain, specifically at the neurotransmitter site that enables one to focus, be attentive, and be patiently decisive. People with hyper-activity actually have less activity in the brain, especially in the areas controlling concentration and impulsivity (like an electrical short). Because AD/HD is a chemical imbalance, medication is used as a form of replacement therapy—replacing or substituting for the chemical that is not there or that is responsible for triggering the body to manufacture these chemicals.

Stimulants strengthen the child's ability to block out external stimuli (irrelevant thoughts and impulses) and to focus attention on what is most important. With medication, the child has the ability to problem solve, thus making the learning process more efficient and concrete. The child is better able to control impulses, thus giving her the ability to make choices in behavior.

The most commonly prescribed psychostimulant for AD/HD is Ritalin (methylphenidate), with the runners-up being Dexadrine (dextroamphetamine), and Cylert (pemoline). Other types of med-ication can also be prescribed, though: the antidepressants Tofranil (imipramine), Norpramin (desipramine), and Zoloft (sertraline); the antihypertensive Catapres (clonidine); and the anticonvulsant Tegretol (carbamazepine). Depending on your child and his symp-tomatic behavior, the doctor may prescribe any one of these, and sometimes more than one.

Because Ritalin is the most widely used, it's the medication I will discuss here. That does not mean it's any better than the other types, but rather that this is not a book on pharmacology. For more information on the other types of medications, you should speak firsthand to your doctor or pharmacist.

The most commonly used form of Ritalin (methylphenidate) comes in short-acting tablets of 5, 10, or 15 milligrams. One dose lasts on average three to four hours. You should start to see some effects within twenty minutes of the child's taking a dosage. It can be prescribed from once a day to three and even four times per day. A timed-release version is available but is not generally con-sidered as effective as the short-acting variety.

Ritalin is usually not taken in the evening, though in some cases an evening dose may be helpful. Some of its effects are the improvement of memory and concentration and enhanced control of frustration and anger. Its two main side effects are sleep disturbances and loss of appetite. Also, there may be a "rebound effect" when the medicine wears off. Rebounding is when the symptomatic behavior returns very suddenly and forcefully.

Ritalin was first prescribed for children with behavior problems in 1937. Since that time it has been researched in depth. As reported by Dr. Russell Barkley, 70 to 80 percent of children with AD/HD respond well to this drug. Although it is a stimulant, it does NOT create a euphoric haze, or "high."

Doctors medicate adolescents for AD/HD about half as often as they do younger children. This lower incidence is the result of doctors' reluctance to prescribe and adolescents' reluctance to take medication. Most of the 20 to 30 percent of cases that aren't successful can be attributed to doctor error in dealing with medication and deliberate deviations from the medication routine by the child or parent. Doctors and centers that specialize in treating AD/HD report a higher success rate of 90 percent.

Dosage depends greatly on your child. There is no set rule for prescribing medication. One doesn't go by height or weight or age. It depends on internal body chemistry, and everyone's works a little differently. For example, my daughter took 5 milligrams of Ritalin three times a day at age five, but my son took 7 ½ milligrams three times a day at age five. For the same reason, two children can need the same dosage but at different time intervals. For example, one child's medication may take four hours to wear off where another's may take only three and a half hours. All of these varying factors only reaffirm the importance of observing your child.

Arriving at the correct dosage requires some trial and error, which is why doctors will prescribe the lowest dosage and build up from there until signs of effectiveness can be seen and/or side effects can be observed. If no negative side effects are observed, the doctor will be able to gradually adjust the dosage until desired effects are obtained. You need to allow at least five days to two weeks before making a determination as to whether or not to adjust the dosage. This enables you to get an accurate and consistent measure of the medication's effectiveness. Also, adjusting the dosage is the doctor's job, not the parent's, child's, or teacher's. Remember, your child should never take medication in a way other than it has been prescribed. And never give medication to someone for whom it hasn't been prescribed.

Fears about Medication

It's natural for us as parents to have fears about our children's taking medication. It's not a quick fix; it's a long-term commitment. But unless we work through these fears objectively, our children may not benefit from a complete treatment plan. Goodness knows, I wasn't proud of choosing medication at first. I was still in the mind-set that "Because I'm not a good enough parent my kids have to take medication." Then I started observing the medicine's effects and educating myself about this disorder. And now I walk around proud that I have the courage to do what's best for my children, even if some people don't approve. You have to be open-minded; otherwise, you and your child will be the ones who suffer the consequences, not those other misinformed, opinionated people.

In looking at our family tree, I noticed that some "branches" showed tendencies toward addictive patterns of behavior, a factor that worried me in using medication as a treatment option. Was I addicting my children to drugs? However, the medicines used to treat AD/HD are not addictive. If anything, kids dislike taking their medicine. They do like the improvement they see in their behavior (that is, the ability to focus and make effective choices) because they realize "Life is much more fun when I'm not in trouble all the time." The child starts feeling better about himself, and his self-esteem goes up, thereby improving his life. Suddenly, the parent begins to notice that the child is much easier to get along with and actually begins to enjoy the child's company.

Although AD/HD may not be as visibly life threatening as other illnesses, it is life threatening because it has such a huge impact on a person's mental and emotional well-being. How many children are injured or even die as the result of impulsive thinking? I wonder how many auto accidents involving teenagers were caused by impulsive thinking and poor judgment? It's a very sobering thought, and suddenly medication doesn't seem to be such a big deal anymore.

Medication Effects

You'll know when medication is effective by observing your child for a four-hour period after medication is given. According to Dr. John Taylor, when you observe your child during this four-hour period, you should notice a dramatic difference in his behavior, characterized by the following effects:

- Activity control—Inappropriate overactivity subsides and coordination improves in the gross and fine motor skills and in the language skills. She isn't interrupting, talking nonstop, or shouting. She's not so clumsy. This is even more noticeable in the school environment.

- Brain in gear—The child is alert, asking questions and able to verbalize appropriately. He's able to use abstract reasoning and logically sequence tasks and ideas. He's not so impulsive, absentminded or scatterbrained—basically, the "gears" in his head are functioning in a normal way.

- Conscience—The child can think responsibly before taking action. She's less attracted to mischief and respects boundaries. Moral judgment improves, and she's more likely to see the harm in an action and respond to it.

- Persistence of effort—The child is more serious about important matters, more helpful, and more considerate of people and things.

- Emotional control—There is a marked decrease in irritability and impatience. He has a normal range of emotional expression and laughs or cries at appropriate times.

- Focus—The child pays attention to what is most important, stays on task, and is able to follow through; she's not so easily distracted.

- Gentleness—Generally, the child is more kind and cooperative toward others; his stubbornness decreases; he accepts guidance and shows a genuinely caring attitude toward others.

When the medication wears off, you will see a return of your child's symptomatic behaviors (hyperactivity, impulsivity, distractibility, etc.). If you don't see any positive effects from the medication, don't worry. It usually just means the dosage needs to be adjusted or that another form of medication would be better suited for your child.

When you give the medication may be as important as how much and what kind. The observations you as a parent make are very valuable when working with your doctor to decide the best times to administer medication. For example, if problems occur in the morning before school, that would be a good time for the first dosage. If your child is a procrastinator, your mornings may go something like this: Wake-up time is 7:00, and school starts at 8:00. This is not a good start. Much goes on from 7:00 to 7:45— her room gets trashed, the bathroom is flooded, and the kitchen looks like a battlefield scene from World War II. Your part in this has consisted of a lot of nagging, yelling, and prodding, but at 7:45 she's sitting in front of the TV, still in pj's, eating a bowl of cereal. In situations like this, a good time for the first dosage would be at 6:30, even if it means waking her up to give it to her.

Signs of Overdosage

Your doctor will likely start at a low dosage and increase from there to eliminate the potential for overdosage. The following indicators suggest a state of overdosage: tics, attention level even lower than the child's normal level of inattentiveness, withdrawal, grogginess, lethargy, depression, or being weepy or overemotional. A state of overdosage means the amount of medication and/or the number of times the medication is taken needs to be reduced. Make your doctor aware of any signs of overmedication right away.

Common Side Effects

As mentioned, Ritalin's two most common side effects are sleep disturbance and decrease in appetite. These problems can be handled in a variety of ways. One option is for the doctor to change the dosage or even the type of medication. I wouldn't recommend the latter, though, unless it's a last resort—especially if the medication is effective in all other respects. Another option you can discuss with your doctor is changing the time you give the medication.

Sleep Disturbance

The side effect of sleep problems can really be frustrating for parents, especially when it's late at night and you've just about had it with your child. (The words "Don't you ever stop?" come to mind.) How you choose to handle this depends on knowing your child's sensitivities and triggers. Also, remember that bedtime is about the time when the last dosage could be wearing off—so you may have to deal with the rebound effect of medication. Changing the timing of medication or sometimes even adding an early evening dosage may help. Adding a dosage will stimulate the neurotransmitter so that the child can focus enough to fall asleep. A child with AD/HD requires twice the amount of time to fall asleep as a "normal" child does—partly because she can't relax her body. Her brain is sending out the message "Stay awake—there's so much to do," even though her body may be telling her, "No, I want to stop." The other side effect—a decrease in appetite—can also be visible at bedtime. In the midst of a rebound effect to medication, the child may be very hungry. Changing the time of medication or giving her a snack prior to or just after medication may help. Again, no changes should be made until you consult your doctor.

Keep in mind that, because bedtime is a transition, incorporating a routine should help. This would include brushing teeth, bathing, putting on pj's, quiet time, and then it's off to bed or tuck-in time. Let the clock do the work for you. A simple reminder that "It's 8:00. What do you need to do now?" works well when you have a routine established. Quiet time is a time for relaxation; this may be something like reading, watching a videotape, or playing quietly— something that helps your child "wind down" instead of "wind up." Quiet time is an important skill for kids with AD/HD to learn. You do have to teach these kids how to relax and how to calm their bodies down.

In other words, bedtime is not the time to be playing touch football. Nor is it a time to be playing video games. For children with AD/HD, video games, while fun and challenging, can be frustrating. They want to get in the screen and make that little guy (or whatever) do what they want him to do, and sometimes they can't. And once the game is shut off, their brains are still going and they need a new outlet for that energy, so they have to move their bodies. Video games can teach focusing capability and eye-hand coordination, but they're something kids with AD/HD should do during the day, not at night before bed. This rule holds true for any activity that raises their level of anxiety or excitability. Start tapering off such activities about an hour or two before bedtime. And activity here does not just refer to physical exertion. If a bubble bath or back rub calms your child down, then do it. On the other hand, if he is overly sensitive to touch, as many kids with AD/HD are, you might want to schedule bath time earlier in the evening.

Something else you can do to help your child learn to relax is to encourage her to keep a journal. What this does is to get all the busy stuff out of her mind so her body can take over and relax long enough to fall asleep. Encourage the child to keep a notebook or journal by her bedside and to write down her thoughts and feelings—the same thoughts and feelings that are keeping her awake. If your child is younger, she can draw pictures instead of write. Writing these things down or drawing them enables her to clear her mind and relax.

Bedtime difficulties could also be about clearly defining boundaries; in this instance, it's the boundary of time. Set bedtime at 9:00 (or whenever) and make an agreement that the child needs to be in bed at this time. He doesn't need to go to sleep, but he needs to be in bed; he can read, draw, listen to music, watch a video, or whatever is agreeable as long as he stays in bed. In this way you are defining the boundary of where his body should be at that time. You can't make your child go to sleep, but you can have the rule that his body needs to be in bed at a specified time. If you have included everything he needs in his bedtime routine, there should be no reason for him to get out of bed. In other words, be proactive when making up this routine and include in it provisions for all the excuses he usually makes to get back up out of bed: I'm hungry, I need a drink, I need to use the bathroom, and so on. And speaking of being hungry, remember he very well could be, if this is about the time his last dosage of medication is wearing off. So include a snack in the bedtime routine.

Tuck-in time is a routine in itself. When my daughter was younger, tuck-in time would go like this: She got in bed, we sang two songs, she said her prayers, and then we had hugs and kisses and said good night. A variation is to have a review of the day's happenings. If you include this review in tuck-in, you need to keep it on track. You can get creative with tuck-ins, but remember to keep them short and sweet. You don't want to drag it out, but you do want it to be long enough to help your child relax. It's also a good idea to avoid naps during the day, if at all possible.

The following two dialogues show how an ineffective bedtime routine looks when compared to an effective bedtime routine.

> Mom: Johnny, it's time for bed now. Stop playing that computer game.
>
> Johnny: Minute, Mom.
>
> Mom: (Ten minutes and a lot of nagging later) That's it! Get into bed now.
>
> Johnny: All right, I'm going! (Still playing game, but has moved a little farther from it.)
>
> Mom: I said now! (Guides—but not gently—child to bed.)
>
> Johnny: Hey, what about my story?
>
> Mom: All right, but just one. (Reads one short story.)
>
> Johnny: Read me another one, pppllleeeaassee! (You guessed it—that was one of those manipulative-type whines.)
>
> Mom: No! I'm not reading another one.
>
> Johnny: You're not very nice! All I asked for was one more! (Boy, he's good! He knows all the right things to say to push Mom's buttons.)
>
> Mom: One more! But that's really it. (This has just sent the message "I didn't really mean what I said the first time.")

The parent now rushes through the second story, says good night, and walks out of the room.

> Johnny: I need a drink. (As he walks back into the family room and sees the computer still on, he starts to think of how he really wants to finish that game.)

> Mom: Get back to bed and go to sleep!

And so on. No wonder the parent feels defeated—this is a nightly battle. By allowing this situation to happen this way, the parent is basically setting herself up for frustration and setting the child up for failure. Let's try it again, only this time with some proactive planning and effective redirecting.

> Mom: Johnny, do you remember the agreement we made earlier today about bedtime? (Touching his arm and making direct eye contact.)

> Johnny: Yeah . . . kind of.

> Mom: We agreed that quiet time starts at 7:00. Guess what? It's 7:00, time to relax. Do you want to read or watch a tape now? (As parent says this, she's guiding him away from the computer and into the other room.)

Johnny decides on a tape; they put it in and he watches it until . . .

> Mom: (Touching his arm and maintaining eye contact) Johnny, you have ten minutes 'till you need to get ready for bed. What do you need to do in ten minutes?

Johnny: Get ready for bed.

Mom: Thanks.

The parent continues with the countdown, repeating this scenario five minutes, then one minute, before bedtime.

Mom: Johnny, it's time to get ready for bed now. (As she states this, she is guiding him away from the TV and into his bedroom, all the while making small talk. She guides him to get his pj's on, brush his teeth, and have a drink, then she waits while he uses the bathroom and guides him toward bed.)

Johnny is now in bed and Mom has just finished reading the agreed-upon one storybook.

Johnny: One more, ppplleeeaassee? (There's that whine again.)

Mom: (Very calmly and matter-of-factly) No, we're done now. You need to stay in bed. What do you need to do now?

Johnny: Stay in bed.

Mom: Thanks. Good night.

The difference in these two scenarios is quite noticeable. Proactive planning was involved in the second, along with gentle guidance and redirection. The parent also spoke much more calmly in the effective scenario. So, even if medication is part of your child's bedtime problems, if you use these tools, bedtime does not have to be a nightly challenge.

Decrease in Appetite

The second most common side effect, a decrease in appetite, affects most children only slightly. The way to work with this is to let your child eat whenever he's hungry—except just before a main meal—and however much he wants. Make sure he has something to eat, whether it's a snack or a meal, before every medication dosage. Dinnertime can be a hassle (whether the child's on medication or not). It's important for me that everyone in the family sit down at the dinner table together; sometimes this is the only time we all see each other. But because of the timing of my daughter's medication, she is not usually interested in dinner. So we've adapted to the situation in a couple of different ways. After school my daughter has a very large snack, almost a regular meal, and then she takes her medication. When she was younger and dinnertime would come, all we would ask of her is to sit with us for at least five minutes and take as many bites of her food as she was old (for example, when she was six she took six bites of something on her plate). One reason I had her take some bites of her dinner is that in our house you don't get dessert unless you eat some dinner (it's another way of following through with consistency). The other reason is that dinnertime is also a time for communication. Even if the child is unable to eat a great amount because of medication, she can participate actively in the conversation. In recent years, we've needed to adapt to a new routine because of my own schedule. What works really well for us now is to have a late dinnertime. By 7:30 or 8:00 my daughter's medication has worn off, and having dinner late eliminates the need for a snack before bed. Sometimes it takes being flexible and adaptable on the parent's part to help things run more smoothly.

As with any situation that involves change in your child's day, be sure to give plenty of warning of the approaching mealtime. That's right—it's another transition. It's a good idea a short time before dinner to invite your child to put away his work and assist you in the process of making dinner. We actually have "Help Mom make dinner" as one of our chore cards to be drawn, lottery-style. This way everyone gets a turn and has some input on the meal that's being made. For whoever doesn't get this card, I utilize the countdown method, giving plenty of notice. Whichever way you choose, the idea here is to "gear up" for dinner. You can also try to make dinner as inviting as possible, incorporating your child's favorite foods whenever possible. Because it is a transition, you can use the same type of effective communication—that is, gentle guidance and a calm voice—illustrated in the effective bedtime dialogue. All you need to do is change the wording.

As far as behavior at the dinner table goes, you need to set clear boundaries of what is acceptable and unacceptable. Before dinner, clearly define what unacceptable behavior consists of and what the consequence will be if the child chooses to act in that way. Be prepared to follow through consistently with that consequence. For example, Dad has spoken to Susie about why she should not play with her food or throw her food at her sister. Susie is very clear about this and knows she can choose to act acceptably by not doing these things. But of course at the dinner table Susie forgets and begins to play with and throw her food. Dad simply and calmly stands up, removes Susie's plate, and states, "When you act like that it tells me you're not ready to eat. When you can show me that you're ready to eat you may have your plate back." Susie looks a little surprised, but then begins to think, "Oh, yeah, I was playing with my food. If I do it again, I'll have to wash dishes tonight. I need to apologize so I can get my plate back."

Your Child's Attitude

The star member of the treatment team, the captain, is your child. He is the key player in all of this and whenever possible needs to be included when decisions are made about the treatment plan. First and foremost, he needs to understand what AD/HD is and how it affects his life. Each team member should be willing and able to talk to the child about this in a way he can comprehend. They should also make him aware of what their roles in all of this are and how they will support him on this team. He, in turn, should be aware of how he can support the other team members (for example, by being honest and open) and what the things are that keep him from doing this (for instance, failing to share information).

If medication is a chosen treatment option, team members should be ready to answer any questions the child may have about it. Whenever a team member communicates with your child, he needs to put it in terms that the child can relate to. An explanation of how AD/HD affects the neurotransmitter responsible for attending to tasks is not going to mean a hill of beans to a five-year-old. Nor will explaining it as a car that needs special gas to help it run better mean a lot to a teenager. As a matter of fact, this type of patronizing would probably turn just about any teen off. There are some great books that help explain AD/HD on various comprehension levels. *Shelley, the Hyperactive Turtle,* by Deborah Moss, and *Otto Learns about His Medicine,* by Matthew Galvin and Sandra Ferrano, are two very good books for younger children. *Putting on the Brakes,* by Patricia Quinn and Judith Stern, is a good one for adolescents and teens. A newsletter by the same name, put out by and for kids with AD/HD, features helpful articles. You can remind older children that some very famous people had AD/HD—Thomas Edison and Winston Churchill, for example. Suggest they read up on these people and see how they worked through their difficulties as youths. The bottom line here is that it's your child's body, and he has a right to know what's going on with it and why.

Most kids who are on medication take it at school because school is often where they most need to focus and control their behavior. Some kids, especially older kids, resist taking their medication at school because they feel ashamed or embarrassed. They are sure no one else at school takes it. (Given the percentage of the population affected by AD/HD, however, I'd be willing to bet this isn't true.) If at all possible, the child should have some say in who administers the medication—the child's teacher, the school nurse, or a school administrator. A lot of kids feel singled out if they have to go to the nurse's office repeatedly to receive medicine.

Most kids willingly accept the idea of medication as part of treatment after an honest explanation of what it does and why it's needed. Some children do object, though, and you need to handle those objections to treatment in the same honest and open manner as you handled the explanation of AD/HD. You need to be willing to listen to your child's point of view. More than likely, her objections are due to unanswered fears or misinformation. Find out what the real issue is, and then address it. Her perception of the situation may be leaving her feeling inadequate, embarrassed, ashamed, or even stupid. She may be feeling inadequate because she is incapable of controlling her behavior. If this is the case, you need to explain that medication doesn't make her outward behavior change. She's the one in charge of that. Medication takes care of the internal functions of attending and focusing, and because of this, she will now have more choice in behavior than she ever did before.

You need to make it very clear that AD/HD is nothing to be ashamed of or embarrassed about. The bottom line is that if you have something that's keeping you from performing at 100 percent, you will more than likely do whatever it takes to compensate for that factor—unless, of course, you enjoy living your life at 50 or 75 percent. I have allergies. If I don't take my medication when they flare up, I pay for it by feeling run down and miserable. If I choose this, I am not living my life at 100 percent; I miss out on things. I have to live with the consequence of feeling rotten, and so does my family—I'm not a very pleasant person to be around at those times. If your child is feeling ashamed or embarrassed about medication or having this disorder, he's basing this on misinformation. It's up to you as the parent to give your child accurate information about AD/HD and its treatment.

Let your child know that you will make every effort to spare him any embarrassment about his medication and that you would never shame him or discuss medication in front of anyone (for example, by saying, "Boy, you're really hyped up today. Go take a pill"). As a parent you are responsible for following through with this commitment.

The child also may be feeling some very real fear. She has only known living with a state of internal chaos. Not having that anymore is like losing a security blanket; it may be a shredded, ragged blanket, but it's what she's used to and, up until this point, all she's had to go on. When you've only known how to live your life one way, it's very scary to switch and live it a different way. I know adults who can't take on this challenge, let alone children. Make it very clear to your child that this new way of living life doesn't have to be scary; it's just different. And just because it's different doesn't mean that it won't be exciting and fun. In all actuality, the person she'll be leaving behind, her old self, was not her real self. The chemical imbalance didn't allow that. Now she has the opportunity to discover who her real self is.

Of great benefit to your child's self-esteem, whether he's having trouble accepting the need for medication or not, is to make him aware of his behavior by contrasting pretreatment to posttreatment behavior. Obviously, you should do this when the child has the ability to focus and comprehend what you're saying to him. What you don't want to do is shame him in any way or make him feel that the pill is the reason for his acceptable, or "good," behavior. Say, for example, that you have just observed your child behaving correctly in an interaction with his sibling. Unless you want to discourage him and make him feel dependent on a pill in order to behave, don't say something like "I'm so proud of you! Boy, am I glad you took your pill so you wouldn't argue with your sister." This would be like taking two steps forward and five steps back. Remember, the goal is to help him recognize that he can now choose to behave effectively, whereas before treatment, he was unable to make that choice. A more effective way, then, of getting your point across would be to say, "I really like the way you handled that situation with your sister. Two months ago you wouldn't have chosen to act that rational with her. You did a great job of negotiating!"

Above all else, don't set your child up with the expectation that medication is going to make her perfect. If you do, you will be setting her up for failure. The one thing we can depend upon in life is change. There is always going to be some new issue that must be addressed and dealt with. If she expects that medication is going to solve all her problems, she will more than likely cast it aside when she doesn't succeed.

Work together with your child and all the members of the treatment team to make this a win-win situation. Impress upon your child the seriousness of following the prescribed treatment plan, and stress that this isn't some whim you are acting upon. This is a very real disorder with very real consequences for his life. And know, too, that the plan you have chosen at first might not be exactly right for all involved. You won't know this, though, unless you are consistent and persistent with the treatment plan. Be willing to commit to it for six months to a year, at which time you can reevaluate. Actually, reevaluating is something I recommend on a yearly basis to everyone, even if the treatment plan does appear successful.

Sometimes children who are not well informed about treatment choose not to take their medication, usually attempting to hide this fact. It will be obvious to everyone when this is happening. In other words, the child's symptomatic behavior will be quite noticeable. If this is the case, take note of it. What was your part in this? Is she in need of more accurate information? Does she have an issue with medication that has not been resolved? Find out the answers to these questions and work proactively with the child to turn the situation around. In the meantime, make it very clear that you are not willing to take part in the consequences of her choice—that is, her symptomatic behavior. When she misbehaves, she will need to get a grip on her behavior.

To repeat, medication is not a substitute for behavior management or good parenting techniques. It's only part of the treatment plan for coping with and compensating for AD/HD. The medications used to treat this disorder are not wonder drugs that will make everything all better. As with any child, there will be good days and bad days. Every child has mood swings, whether or not he has AD/HD and whether or not he is on medication. Everyone is entitled to a bad day from time to time. If your child seems to have made that choice, take note of it. Do some observation and think about the things that could have helped trigger that choice—for example, lack of sleep, feeling emotionally drained, overactivity (activity that stimulates him to the point of no return), or a tough day at school. In your observation journal, make a note of any of these triggers, and try to relax—this too shall pass. In the future, see what you can do to prevent these things from happening.

Chapter 6

What's So Hard about School?

Often, children with AD/HD are not diagnosed until problems show up in school. AD/HD can wreak havoc on academic performance, though not all children with the disorder have noticeable difficulties early on academically. At some point, though, these problems will make themselves evident. These difficulties are not necessarily the result of an inability to learn, but rather the inability to obtain and process information. These processes are vital because information builds upon itself, accumulating day by day, month by month, year by year. So it's critical that AD/HD and the challenges it presents be addressed as early as possible. And because areas of difficulty vary from child to child, the areas have to be pinpointed in order to design an effective teaching program.

Once in school, children with AD/HD face a variety of academic and social challenges, some of which they will not have encountered at home. They are asked to be organized, sit still, follow directions, be attentive, control their impulses, and demonstrate motor control. They may experience difficulty at one or more of the following times: starting tasks, staying on task, completing tasks, making transitions, interacting with others, following through on directions, producing work at consistently normal levels, and organizing multistep tasks. Children with this disorder can have difficulty with one or all parts of the attention process. They may have difficulty choosing something on which to focus their attention. Or they may have difficulty selecting which thing or task needs their attention at that specific moment. Once the object or task has been chosen and singled out, they may have trouble sustaining attention for as long as is needed. They may have trouble shutting out other stimuli that distract them from the task. Or these children may be unable to switch gears from one task to the next.

These demands, which are virtual requirements for school success, are difficult enough for a "normal" child, let alone one with AD/HD. And with each passing year the demands steadily increase. Because of the structure of a preschool environment, many children who have AD/HD aren't diagnosed until the first grade. If they aren't detected at this point, the next peak time for diagnosis is third grade, when reading and organization begin to become increasingly difficult. Also, at this time they are expected to work independently, and teachers at this level are less tolerant of restlessness and "off task" behavior. Some children even make it to middle school before they are detected. This is another prime time for diagnosis because of the difficulties a new structure and changing classes present. These children may have had some problems all along, but they were more than likely attributed to immaturity, with the hope that they would be outgrown. Or they may have come from an elementary school that was either highly structured or unconsciously adaptable in meeting their needs. In the meantime, they have fallen further behind academically with each passing year and suffered many failures and social rejections, and thus developed a poor self-image.

THE PARENT-TEACHER RELATIONSHIP

As I noted in chapter 5, the child's teacher plays a very valuable role on the treatment team—that of academic advisor. This role is one of effective observer, educator, and evaluator. This would include, but not be limited to, adapting or adjusting the curriculum, building self-esteem and social skills, and monitoring treatment in regard to the child's academic career. It does not include diagnosis. Teachers are not mental health professionals and should not be expected to perform in this capacity, nor should they take it upon themselves to do this. However, next to the parents, they have the greatest amount of interaction with the child, as well as a great amount of influence. Their close relationship with the child allows them to play a very personal role on the treatment team.

As I am writing this, an interesting thought comes to mind. The main descriptive features of the role of academic advisor could easily apply to another team member—the parent. In a way, teachers do serve as our surrogates. Being a teacher myself, I can tell you that next to parenting a child with special needs, teaching one deserves more acknowledgment than it gets. I remember seeing a poster once that I thought summed it up very well. It said, "If educators received the financial support that the Pentagon gets, and the Pentagon was financially dependent on bake sales, the world would be a much more peaceful place."

I'm not suggesting we put teachers on pedestals. I am merely saying that they play a very important role in our children's lives. Let's not take that for granted. We need to be supportive of them in their endeavor by developing an effective working relationship with them.

DEVELOPING AN EFFECTIVE RELATIONSHIP

You go about developing an effective relationship with your child's teacher just as you would with other members of the treatment team. The tools and techniques for relationship building presented so far are all applicable to this relationship. As I mentioned previously, though, your relationship with this team member takes on a more personal dimension than your relationships with the other team members. It's quite common when you have a personal relationship with someone to have differing viewpoints. It's the same in this relationship. You have your perspective, the teacher has her perspective, and then we throw in that rather uncommon little denominator, your child, and her perspective. What's important to remember here is that each person's perspective is valid. It's that person's reality. It's not right or wrong—it just is.

But if we all see things from different angles, how can we work toward a common goal? Easy. Be willing to see things from others' points of view without necessarily giving up your own. More than likely this will broaden your own perspective, and it certainly will help you work much more effectively together. Also, remember that in order to achieve a goal, it takes the effort of all team members. If it didn't, you'd be able to do the work all by yourself. You'd be self-sufficient and already have all of the information you needed. Obviously, in this case that plan won't succeed. You need the input of the other team members; you need the ability to see things from their perspectives. Just as you have valuable information that is not evident to them from their relationship with your child, their viewpoints hold valuable information for you.

Environmental surroundings influence how we perceive kids with AD/HD. As I have mentioned before, the interactions and behaviors of kids with AD/HD are, to an extent, a response to the environment. Parents and teachers interact with these children in very contrasting environments. I'd be willing to bet that your home does not bear a great resemblance to a classroom. I think it's also a safe bet that your child's classroom does not share a great number of similarities with your home. The fact is, they shouldn't. They serve different needs. They may resemble each other, though, in how they incorporate structure or in their ability to adapt.

Your child may show symptomatic behavior of AD/HD more at home, more at school, or evenly at both. It depends on which environment is more able to adapt in meeting his needs. Usually, though, when parents and teachers have differing perceptions of the child's behavior, it's the teacher who's encountering the majority of difficulties. This is because most school environments are not conducive to someone with AD/HD. And that's not meant as a derogatory remark. It's just a fact. It's standard practice to find bright posters on every available piece of wall space. It's common to find mobiles and fluorescent lighting, which distract people with AD/HD. It's standard to find an ample supply of manipulatives and a variety of classroom pets. It's standard to find large, uncovered windows with desks angled for optimum viewing. Add a child with AD/HD to this environment and you get the equivalent of a kid in a candy shop.

It's understandable why standard formats are used in creating a classroom environment. They have a proven track record, at least with kids who aren't affected by AD/HD. Teachers also tend to follow proven methods of teaching. They attempt to reach and teach the most receptive kids and use what energy is left to work with those kids who don't fall within the norm. For a teacher, this is a very understandable attitude; it's safe and realistic. But there are alternative methods that are equally as realistic, though maybe not quite as popular. And this last part, the unpopularity, is what makes them seem unsafe to teachers. It's much easier to go with the flow than to stand out and be different. I applaud the teacher who dares to be different, who goes against the norm for the betterment of every child in the classroom and not just the ones most easily reached. For the child who has AD/HD, or any type of learning impairment, this teacher is a lifesaver. He doesn't see the child as a threat to the status quo of the classroom or to his capabilities as a teacher. Rather, he sees the child as he does all children, as a unique individual with certain characteristics that only she can share with the classroom. This is the teacher who enjoys the opportunity to individualize a child's education. He is the rare educator who celebrates the uniqueness of each and every child in his care.

I have been fortunate enough to teach in schools that promote this type of practice, that actually expect this type of teacher to be the standard. The benefits for the children are obvious. They all thrive in this type of environment, not just the kid with special needs. I've also been fortunate enough to experience the "old school" type of teacher, through my own education and now the education of my children. I say fortunate not to be sarcastic but rather to emphasize that I am glad that I've experienced that teaching style. Otherwise I'd never know exactly what I don't want my own teaching style to be. Nor would I know what does not work for my children as far as teaching goes. In retrospect, I see my experience with these teachers as an opportunity.

Let me give you a real-life example of this, although I won't use the real names of the people involved. It was the first conference between a kindergarten teacher and one of her student's parents. It seems the little boy, whom I'll refer to as Sam, wasn't following the norm. He was having difficulty staying on task. The teacher knew that the child was taking Ritalin, and not having a great deal of information about this or the child, she automatically assumed that his difficulties in class were due to the Ritalin and not the work in class. When Sam was asked how he was doing in school or how he liked his class, he would respond, "It's boring—it's bad." Let's take a closer look at Sam's history. Now six, he had been in a classroom environment since the age of one and a half. His mother was a teacher fortunate enough to work at a school that allowed her to bring him to its preschool class. The school encouraged this type of practice to reinforce the concept of family. So at the time of this conference, the boy had been in school for four and a half years. In that time no teacher had ever noticed or encountered any negative or unproductive behavior.

Because of his early birthdate Sam was unable to enter the private school's kindergarten with his classmates. His mother, faced with the choice of letting him attend another year of preschool or placing him in a public school kindergarten program for one year until he met the age requirement of the private school, opted for the latter—that is, for her son to attend kindergarten for two years, one in the public school and one in the private school. In his first year of kindergarten her son had excelled. His teacher was one of those exceptional educators who wasn't threatened by going against the norm. By the time that year ended Sam was reading at a first-grade level. So what was the problem? According to his academic history, he should have been doing well.

The mother asked the new kindergarten teacher, the one in the private school, just what it was that he was experiencing difficulty with, thinking that maybe she needed to adjust his dosage of medication. (By the way, Sam had been diagnosed at age three and then reevaluated at age five with all test results conclusively showing AD/HD.) It seemed Sam wasn't spending enough time with his math work. What was the math work he was being asked to do? Coloring circles. It wasn't hard to figure out that the problem was not medication but boredom. He had been coloring circles for the last four and a half years, and the teacher wondered why he couldn't stay on task. Thinking maybe Sam's teacher wasn't aware of his previous year in kindergarten, his mother brought it to her attention and suggested that maybe while the other children were coloring, Sam could do something a little more challenging. The teacher's response was "That would mean I'd have to individualize his work." Now that's a thought!

How was this resolved? After hearing the teacher's response, the parent knew what kind of year she and her child would likely have and accepted the fact that it would just be a means of passing time until her child entered first grade. In order for Sam to stay interested in learning, she would have to work with him at home. From past and present observations by her son's treatment team members she knew that this was not a question of his medication. But she also knew that the healthy thing to do was to do her part in establishing a good working relationship with Sam's teacher.

To make it clear that the Ritalin was not the factor making it hard for Sam to stay on task, the parent suggested a two-week trial without medication while Sam was in the classroom. Then they would reevaluate the situation. During this trial the effects of Sam's AD/HD were quite apparent to everyone in his life: He became very hyperactive and began acting out—hitting, kicking, shouting, and so on. At the end of the trial period, the parent met with the

147

teacher and asked if Sam's ability to stay on task had improved. Although the deterioration in Sam's behavior must have been obvious to her, the teacher's response was "Well, no—but I think he's happier." She might as well have said, "Well, no—but I'm happier because I don't have to adapt to the reality of Sam's problems in my class." The parent shared with her others' observations of Sam's behavior during those two weeks and stated that Sam would need to go back to his treatment plan.

THREE SIDES TO EVERY STORY

You've heard the expression "There are always two sides to every story." When you factor in the element of a child with AD/HD, you need to make that three sides: the parent's, the teacher's, and the child's. In order for this child to be successful and for everyone to work together effectively, we have to be able to see one another's viewpoints. That, again, doesn't mean we will all agree, but that unless you look at the situation from every angle you're not going to get a clear picture of what's really going on. There are some things you can do to enhance this process of seeing things from others' viewpoints.

The Teacher

Teachers are trained and experienced in the areas of childhood development and education, but the parents are the experts on their particular child. Teachers need to realize what a valuable store of information parents have about their child. Specifically, teachers must be willing to talk to the parents and get to know the child's strengths and weaknesses, her likes and dislikes, and the triggers associated with her AD/HD. All of this information will be very valuable when working with the child.

It is also important for teachers to remember that parents have a huge emotional investment in their child. The teacher more than likely only has the child for one year, but the parents have a lifelong commitment—as a result, the parents have much more at stake than the teacher does. The school environment can also be quite intimidating to some parents. A parent-teacher conference can be as stressful as a teacher's performance review—the tension so thick you can cut it with a knife. The teacher can help put parents at ease by understanding that, when parents do become emotional, it's not meant personally. Being a teacher myself, I know it can be difficult to keep in mind where the parents are coming from, but it is very important.

It also helps everyone for the teacher to focus on the child's strengths. If a teacher's communication consists only of a detailed listing of the child's weaknesses, negative points, and failures, the parents are not going to feel supported. Granted, it's very easy for a teacher to become discouraged and frustrated with a child who has AD/HD. But parents' morale needs a good booster shot every now and then, too. This doesn't mean ignoring the child's weaknesses; it just means making parents aware of the positive as well as the negative. This is for the teacher's benefit as much as the parents' because it is a good reminder that even the smallest of tasks may be a major accomplishment for a child with AD/HD.

The Parents

Parents can enhance the parent-teacher relationship by considering the teacher's perspective. Don't be too quick to assume that when things aren't going well it's automatically the teacher's fault. You play a big part in this, too. As parents, we have a tendency to think that our children should be more important than others in the eyes of the teacher. Sometimes our demands are a bit unrealistic. Children affected by AD/HD do need special assistance to function successfully in school, but this assistance doesn't necessarily mean constant intervention on the teacher's part. Under normal circumstances a teacher has to meet the demands of thirty or so other children, sixty or so parents, and several other staff members. In certain situations it may be more realistic to address your concerns to an appropriate staff member (for example, problems with medication at school may be handled with the school nurse). But remember to keep the teacher informed of any changes made in the treatment plan.

Remember also that your child's teacher is with your child a great deal of the time. The teacher's insights can be very valuable to the treatment team. You need to make every effort to let the teacher know that you appreciate him, that he's a valued member of the treatment team, and that you will support him to the best of your abilities in working with your child.

Behavior problems that seem too insignificant to bother with to the parent may represent major challenges to the teacher in the classroom environment. There are three sides to the situation, remember: yours, the teacher's, and the child's. Children with AD/HD have great difficulty interpreting their own behavior and that of others. Your child's memories of the situation may not be 100 percent accurate.

It's great when your child gets a teacher with whom everything just "clicks." It's not so great when this doesn't happen. A child with AD/HD can quickly drain the energy of even the most dedicated, patient, and persistent of teachers. In a classroom of thirty or so children, having even just one child who is constantly creating disruptions and making excessive demands on her time can be disheartening. The child's behavior also tends to have a ripple effect on the other children, distracting them from their work. This child may be very aggressive, causing the teacher to worry not only about how the child's behavior affects the other children's academic progress, but also about their physical safety. In these cases, it's understandable why she might feel frustrated and her capabilities challenged.

Just as you can't use regular parenting techniques with this child, you also have to approach teaching the child from a whole new perspective. If your child's teacher expresses a concern, be willing to listen objectively. Empathize with her and volunteer your services in working through the difficulty, and ask if she would be willing to work with you. A possible solution would be to have the teacher work with the child on the difficulty at school and for you to follow up on it at home. You can do this by using a home-school checklist (discussed later in this chapter), backed up by positive reinforcement and logical consequences. Above all, remember that you, your child, and the teacher are all on the same team, working toward a common goal.

The Child

In essence, a child with AD/HD does not feel she is out to get you, but rather that you and the rest of the world are out to get her. She feels picked on, disliked, and that life is not fair. In chapter 1, I mentioned a study done at Michigan State University by Dr. Maria Rohrkemper with a group of elementary school children. In that study the "normal" children said that the child they saw in the video could have controlled his behavior and that the teacher was just doing her job by correcting him. But the children with AD/HD saw it completely opposite. They said that the child could not control his behavior and should not be held accountable for it, and that the teacher was overreacting because she didn't like the child. This clearly shows that a child with AD/HD doesn't understand how her behavior affects her classmates. For example, if she pokes others as she walks by their desks, she probably doesn't even realize she's doing it, and if she does, she is unaware of its effects on others. The teacher can point out the behavior, make the child aware of its effects, and think of a constructive way to counter it—for example, saying, "When you poke people as you walk by them, it bothers them. They can't concentrate on their work, and sometimes it even hurts. Next time how about putting your hands in your pockets as you walk by them? Does that work for you? . . . Great!"

I tried an interesting experiment in my own home along these lines. Frustrated and at the end of my rope, I knew of no way to point out the effects of my children's behavior other than to use a tape recorder. For about half an hour I recorded our interactions discussing chores. The discussion turned into a "he said, she said" argument. When I played the recording to my kids, they responded, "I don't remember saying that, but I guess I did." My purpose was not to make somebody wrong but to utilize an unbiased third party—the tape recorder—as a sort of mediator.

It is crucial not only to keep your child's self-esteem intact, but also to strengthen it. Criticizing and shaming only defeat this purpose. Make use of positive encouragement and reinforcement for being prompt or getting an assignment done on time. Encouraging statements should be made on the basis of the process rather than the product. Use statements like "I like the way that you proofread your own paper" rather than "You're so smart." Accept the child on the basis of his own qualities. Every person on the face of this earth has great value and importance, and a grade or an award is not necessarily proof of that value and importance. We as parents need to remember the difference between supporting our children and pressuring them to achieve, which is a form of perfectionism. Don't compare your child to any other child. No two people are alike, so why waste time and bruise your child's self-esteem by comparing him to someone else. If you have certain expectations of your child, make sure they are positive ones. Many people with AD/HD have learned to cope and compensate quite well and are very, very successful.

COMMUNICATION LINKS

Communication among everyone on the treatment team is important, but it is particularly important between the teacher and the parents, as they have the most interaction. It's important to have realistic expectations, though. Teachers and parents, as well as everyone on the treatment team, are all subject to the demands of today's society. It's common for family concerns to take a back seat to work schedules. Teachers need to remember that parents may both be employed full-time outside of the home. Parents need to remember that teachers have a life outside of school.

Communication between school and home can occur in a variety of ways, each with its pluses and minuses. Some ways that I find to be of great benefit are conferences, telephone conversations, notes, home visits (rare nowadays), and school visits. E-mail is also a great way to communicate because it's less intrusive than a phone call but more immediate than a note or a school visit. It's a good idea to meet with your child's teacher early in the school year to agree on the methods you will use.

Conferences can strengthen the parent-teacher relationship, but both team members need to prepare and plan ahead for these. Make sure you have copies of any relevant paperwork you plan on discussing: report cards, notes sent home, some of her work that you may have a question about, and some of her work that you thought was terrific (this not only lets the teacher know you are aware of your child's strengths but also that you appreciate his). Bring your observation journal, and if you've been working with behavioral checklists, bring those, too. That way you can compare notes with the teacher. If the teacher has been keeping track of his observations or utilizing behavioral checklists, he should have those handy.

The telephone can serve you in a couple of ways. It's good for "emergency" conferences when an issue comes up that needs to be dealt with before a face-to-face meeting can be arranged. You can also use the telephone to issue a quick warning that the child is having an unusually bad day. In this way the teacher can prepare herself for working with the child accordingly. After school is a good time to let the teacher know, via an occasional call, that the child had a great day and you appreciate the effort on her part. The teacher can also communicate with you in this way. A word of warning, though: Telephone calls between home and school shouldn't happen every day unless there are extenuating circumstances.

Home visits are a great way for the teacher to observe how the child interacts in an environment other than school. If the teacher hasn't had the child in her classroom yet, a home visit allows the two of them to get to know each other in an environment that is familiar and not so intimidating to the child. These are quite difficult for the teacher to arrange, however, because of the number of students in the classroom. From the teacher's viewpoint, though, it is a good idea to meet a child who has AD/HD before school starts, even if it's not possible to meet with all of the students in the class. This way the teacher can prepare herself and the child for the upcoming transition.

School visits are vital for parents. Make a commitment to yourself to observe the classroom your child will be in, before placement if possible. I question any school that doesn't allow classroom observation, and, in fact, wouldn't put my child in a room that was not open to my observation. As a former teacher, I would welcome the opportunity to show off my room. A good way to approach this is for you to offer your services as an aide in the classroom. Realize that if you are present in the classroom while your child is there, his behavior will not necessarily reflect his normal interactions in the room, but you'll still be able to observe the other interactions and workings of the room. It's critical for you to use the tool of observation whenever possible in order to know what you're dealing with.

The school should allow parents access to the school's resource room and to information on programs offered, as well as give explanations of what approaches are being implemented and why, why certain materials are or aren't being used with the child, and why the child is or isn't learning. The parent in turn needs to make clear what the school can realistically expect of the child. Otherwise, the school staff could use the wrong approach. You need to familiarize yourself with what each staff member does with your child. It's a good idea to keep track of all of this information and any information about your child's academic career in a notebook or file. This information can then serve as a reference point not only for yourself but for any future school personnel.

When the need arises for very close communication between school and home the best approach is to use a home-school checklist like the one shown on the next page. This report can be sent to and from school every day and allows the parent to know how the child's day went and the teacher to know how his evening and morning went. (It can also be used as a weekly report: "My Week Was . . ."). In this way, parent and teacher can both work on target behaviors such as completing class work or cooperatively playing on the playground. The parent can provide a backup system at home, such as enforcing daily privileges based on school performance. These privileges should be separate from privileges earned by behavior in the home environment, or else they will have little meaning. As with any system you employ, this has to be done daily and consistently. It will make no sense to the child if you try to work on a behavior that occurred a week ago; children with AD/HD literally live in the moment and in that moment only.

Something that has really helped me as a parent, and my child and her teacher, is the daily work plan that her teacher has implemented for all of the children in the class. Because every child is involved, no one feels singled out. Every morning my daughter gets a slip of paper with eight "works" for her to do that day. Each time she finishes a work the teacher initials her work plan. Some days she gets all eight done, and some days she doesn't. On the days she doesn't, I know from the plan what she needs to work on at home, and she knows exactly what she has to do the following morning. At the end of the week her teacher sends home a summary of the week's work. This helps me help her.

Ideally, team members will be available to one another at any given time—within reason. There will be times when one member of the team is going to need to confer with another member

---

SAMPLE HOME-SCHOOL CHECKLIST

Name_____ Date _____

My Day Was . . .

☐ Great ☐ Fine ☐ Challenging

Teacher Comments	Yes	No
Showed cooperation	_____	_____
Stayed on task	_____	_____
Completed required class work	_____	_____
Completed required homework	_____	_____

Target behavior:

Strengths:

Challenges:

Assignments/tests:

Teacher signature _____

Parent signature _____

Parent or teacher comments:

---

on short notice. Be open to this, remembering that the other team member more than likely has a genuine concern that needs to be shared. The key to keeping a good line of communication open, however, is for no one team member to overdo it. Being excessive means being overprotective. Daily notes and occasional phone calls are good; daily notes, daily phone calls, weekly conferences, and so on are excessive, if not obsessive. Your goal is merely to provide information and allow the other team member to work with it. If you can't do this, you are denying that person the right to be valuable.

WHAT TO DO ABOUT HOMEWORK

Homework sounds reasonably simple, right? You bring some work home, you sit down and do it, and you turn it in the next day. As kids say today: Not! For us, yes, but for a child with AD/HD daily homework can be a traumatic experience. He's not focused enough to write down the assignment, so he forgets what to do. Or he copies down the assignment, but it takes so much energy for him to focus that he doesn't know what he actually has to do with the assignment because that explanation occurred while he was still focusing on writing it down. Or he writes it down, understands it, but misplaces it. He forgets the books or equipment necessary to complete the assignment. When he gets home, he procrastinates, putting the work off for as long as possible while his parents continue to nag at him to get it done. Once he actually sits down to do it, his mind wanders and he does all kinds of other work instead. A parent needs to stand guard over him, and the process drags on for hours, or he'll rush through it, resulting in work that looks like it's been through a blender. When he gets back to school he realizes he has forgotten his masterpiece at home, or he has it but he forgets to turn it in. Doesn't sound too successful, does it? Not only is this overwhelming for the child, it's also overwhelming for parents and teachers who don't know where to start. The chart on the next page shows common homework stumbling blocks and briefly notes the stepping stones that can help kids with AD/HD deal with homework. I'll discuss these in the following pages.

What's the Assignment?

There are ways to help the child be clear about what an assignment is and what it entails. One way is for the teacher to create homework teams. She pairs up the children in the room, putting kids with AD/HD with more organized kids, and has them go over the assignments for that day before they go home. A homework partner or teammate can help the child understand the assignment. It's best if all the children in the room have a partner so certain children don't feel singled out. Many teachers implement this idea by using homework groups instead of partners. At the end of the day the groups get together and review the assignments. Other teachers use an entirely different technique—the signal card. This is a card that only the teacher and child know about. They have a preestablished agreement that when the teacher flashes or holds the card the child then knows to focus and write down the assignment.

It's also a good idea for the teacher to provide all children with a weekly or monthly assignment sheet. This eliminates the "What is she going to make us do tonight?" dilemma. The teacher should also provide students with a calendar for the year showing any long-term assignments—just saying "due in six weeks" has no meaning for a child who has AD/HD. I should state, too, that when I say, "provide assignment sheets," that also means to send a copy in the mail to the parents.

Getting Organized

Just as you would modify any behavior, you will need to start with one task at a time when working with homework problems.

HOMEWORK: STUMBLING BLOCKS
TO STEPPING STONES

Doesn't realize assignment being given	Use special helper, signal card
Doesn't write assignment down	Use special helper, assignment calendar
Doesn't understand assignment	Use special helper, signal card
Doesn't bring homework home	All or extra textbooks at home
Doesn't arrive home with homework	All or extra textbooks at home, no stops on the way
Doesn't start homework	Homework routine, rule—work before play
Doesn't complete homework	Frequent check-ins
Doesn't check homework	Proofreading and positive reinforcement
Doesn't put homework away	Organized notebook, homework routine
Doesn't take homework back to school	Strategic placement, homework routine
Loses homework at school	Organized notebook
Forgets to hand homework in	Special helper, signal cards

If your child always forgets her books, get a second set for home. You may be able to borrow these from the school, or you may have to buy them. Make it a rule, too, that there are to be no stops on the way home from school—come directly home. This way books and assignments don't get left somewhere else.

Help the child organize his schoolwork by providing him with a three-ring binder as a central workbook. Structure it like this: Divide it into sections, one for each subject and an extra one for doodling. In each section have loose-leaf paper, and in the front put a plastic pencil case to hold pens, pencils, stapler, staples, erasers, markers, a hole punch, and lunch money. On the front inside cover tape an assignment sheet; on the back inside cover glue a manila envelope for all loose assignments or notes to teacher or parent. By using the binder the child eliminates the problem of which notebook to bring home and when, as well as the problem of leaving his work somewhere while finding a pencil or some glue. It's all right there in one book. And when he leaves school he only needs to remember one notebook instead of three or four. The hole punch in the pencil case is important because every handout he gets can be punched and put immediately into its subject area. Anything he needs to take home goes right in the envelope on the back cover. All assignments are written down on the sheet on the front inside cover.

When the child finishes her homework at night, have a designated spot for it, her books, and her backpack by the front door so she literally can't miss it. Some parents even find it necessary to put these items right in front of the door so the door won't open until the child picks them up, or right on top of her shoes. Be strategic. Something that has worked well in our home is to have a "book-bag bin." It's a milk crate that sits next to our front door. The rule is you don't get any farther when you come home until the book-bag is put in the bin. It doesn't come out of the bin until homework time, when it goes straight to the child's desk. When she's finished it goes straight back into the bin; otherwise homework isn't considered finished. She can't go play until it's in the bin. In the beginning this may take some reminders. When you see your child is finished with her homework remind her where she needs to put her books. Make it part of the homework routine. You can also include a "check" in the bedtime routine—before she goes to bed she checks that her things are ready for the morning.

Implement the rule of work before play, especially if your child is a procrastinator. If he needs to release some energy when he gets home from school, as most kids with AD/HD do, that's fine. Let him have an hour to blow off steam, but then follow through with the homework routine. There is no more play or free time until the homework is done. Once you have an established homework or afternoon routine, this step is quite simple.

Structuring the Homework Area

Your child will need an organized, structured area to do her homework in. This is another way to set her up to be successful. She needs to study at the same time and in the same place every day. In the beginning, that will be the goal to work toward. Try to make it in an out-of-the-way place that's free from household traffic or distractions. It needs to be set up ahead of time and ready to go when homework time comes, with all the materials she needs—pens, pencils, erasers, paper, markers, scissors, whatever—so she won't have to stop and get up and look for things. Store all of the materials in one place—a drawer in her desk or a crate next to it. Make sure the lighting is good. Some people with AD/HD are sensitive to the buzzing and glare of fluorescent lamps (this is due to their hypersensitivity). Thus, it may be helpful for your child to use a reading lamp at her desk instead of using overhead lighting.

You may even find it helpful to place some sort of cubicle structure around the desk. This doesn't have to be elaborate; it may just be a matter of placing a large, three-sided piece of cardboard around the desk.

Chapter 6

The Homework Routine

It's important to incorporate a homework routine as early as possible into your child's education. With younger children, this may just be a time for reading or listening to a story tape. The idea here is to create and establish a pattern for studying. If your child is older, it may take more time to get this routine established. Set a time for study, the same time every day, and stick to it. By observing how your child's afternoon normally goes you'll be able to tell when the best time in his day will be to establish a homework routine. Some children need to exert some physical energy when they get home from school. If this is the case with your child, you may want to schedule homework time for early in the evening, perhaps right after dinner. This is also a good time if both parents are working outside the home. If your child is the world's greatest procrastinator, you may want to schedule homework time for immediately after school—no playtime until study time is done. It's a good idea for your child to have a snack just before sitting down to do homework. This alleviates the "Mom, I can't study because I'm hungry" syndrome. Kids with AD/HD tend to have better study habits on a full stomach.

After the child sits down at his desk, be prepared—in the beginning especially—to help him make the work more manageable. After spending eight hours at school the thought of more schoolwork is overwhelming to these children. Show your child that the situation is manageable by breaking tasks down into smaller steps. Depending on your child's work habits, you may want to start with the biggest or hardest task and work toward the smallest or easiest task. Have him review the assignments to figure out which he would like to do first; then plan the order for doing the rest. He also needs to check his long-term assignment calendar for work that he may need to be doing on that. Once he's got a work plan established, let him go to it. Be there to guide, but avoid any hovering or nagging instinct you may have. Remember, you're not his supervisor; you're his parent. And you are not there to do the work for him. Once when I was teaching, I overheard two parents discussing the recent science fair projects. I thought it was funny when one said to the other, "What did you get on your project? I got an A," and the other said, "I got a B." These were supposed to be the children's projects. Remember, your child didn't learn to walk by your doing it for him, and he won't learn to do his schoolwork if you do it for him either.

Feedback is also a part of this process. Make sure the directions on assignments are clear to the child before she begins. If they are not, read them to her, and then have her repeat back what she heard. You may need to take this a step further and have her read some of the questions to you. If she's not clear on their meaning, you may have to summarize for her. This is especially helpful for younger children who are just getting into the homework process. Now that you've got her started, let her go. Periodically check in on her. You may need to stay in the same room but occupied with other things, or you may be able to work on something else in another room and come back from time to time to check in. This depends on the level of focusing capability your child has.

How Much Is Too Much?

By the time he's in fourth grade your child will likely be studying about an hour at home every day. Even if he doesn't have any assignments to do, he can spend the time reading and reviewing, or doing workbooks or at-home projects. It's a good idea to start with short homework sessions and gradually build up to longer ones. It's also a good idea to include break times in the sessions. After about thirty minutes of studying, have the child take a five-minute break. Give him a two-minute warning, and when that's up, guide him back to work. Gradually, as he gets older, you can build up to an hour before taking a break. The idea here is to increase the amount of time spent focusing so that by the time he's writing term papers in high school his body and brain will be used to focusing for a good period of time—that is, approximately two hours.

If your child spends far more or far less time studying than this, you need to stand back and observe the process in detail. If she's procrastinating, you may want to look at how often you are checking in. You also may want to enlist the help of some encouragement aids—charts for progress, privileges granted after work is complete, and so on. If she's speeding right through the process, you will probably need to help her slow down and focus on details, such as spelling and neatness. You'll also need to help her realize the importance of comprehending the material studied.

If your child's homework process is dragging out because he truly does not understand the assignment, or he is bringing home work that he didn't complete in school plus his assigned homework, you need to speak to the teacher. Homework means a review of the work done at school; it does not mean learning new things at home that should have been learned in school.

Staying on Task

The biggest help to keep your child on task is a structured environment free from any unnecessary external stimuli. Things like TV, a ringing telephone, the sounds of dinner being made, or even sitting in a wobbly chair can prove very distracting to this child. On the other hand, some people with AD/HD can concentrate better if there is some sort of "white noise" in the background. A fan running, a sound machine, or even listening to the same music tape every time he studies can serve to block out other external stimuli.

There are various other methods you can use to keep your child on task with his homework. These are basically the same tools you would use to keep him on task with any work or activity he is involved in. One way is to use intermittent check-ins. When your child is doing something relatively new it's a good idea to "pop in" every five to ten minutes, depending on the task. Be willing to make yourself available without standing guard. If you feel it's necessary, you can use reinforcements like positive feedback or some type of point system, rewarding him after so many points are earned. Another way I mentioned previously is to have the rule of work before play.

You can also work with your child as a teacher would (or should). Break down the tasks into small steps. Each time a step is completed she can move on to the next step, and she doesn't need to worry about the next step until the previous step is completed. Also, through your observations you can sequence the tasks according to her needs. In other words, if she has more focusing capability at the end of study time, save the work that requires the most attention until the end. If her confidence level is higher at the beginning of study time, have her tackle the most difficult tasks first. You can also vary the tasks like this: easy, hard, easy, hard, and so forth. Knowing your child and how she works most efficiently will help you make these adjustments.

A couple of other things you can do to compensate for distractibility are afternoon medication and using an attention tape. Afternoon medication consists of giving your child a second or third dosage after he is home. You will need to talk with your doctor about this, but if your child appears to need an extra dosage to complete his homework, it's definitely worth looking into.

An attention tape is a tape recording that you can make yourself to help keep your child on task. It could be a hindrance or a help, depending on your child. What you do is this: Get a tape recorder and something to produce a tone, such as a spoon tapping on a water glass. Start the tape, wait a few seconds, and say, "Begin." At one-, two-, or three-minute intervals, sound the tone, continuing this process for the rest of the tape. What your child does is this: She starts the tape at the beginning of her study time. When she hears the tone she asks herself, "Was I paying attention to what I'm doing?" If so, she places a check mark on a sheet of paper. At the end of study time she adds up all of the checks. If you have a reinforcer system already established you can use it with the attention tape and tie in a reinforcer depending on the number of checks she has.

Comprehension

Now your child is doing the work—but is he comprehending it? One way to check is to incorporate the use of feedback, both on your part and his part. When my daughter (a first grader at the time) was required to do a history project along with all of her schoolmates, I was bound and determined that it would not be my project, but hers. As it was her first experience doing a large project she was very excited, and I wanted to keep that enthusiasm level high. We went to the library, and I showed her how to look for the books she would need. She chose a few and I chose a few that looked relevant to her topic. We spent the next few evenings reading to each other from these books, incorporating a lot of feedback into the process. I would ask her to tell me in her own words what she had read, and she would do the same with me. At first we went literally sentence by sentence—we'd take a sentence and put it in our own words and then go on. Gradually, we built up to paragraph by paragraph. At this stage she was able to dictate to me the meaning or thought in the passage she had just read. After a few pages of dictation—double-spaced and in large writing so she could read it herself—we had a report. So that she also took part in the writing process, she spent the next week copying every-thing I had transcribed in her own writing. It took her about fif-teen minutes a night for five nights to finish this. Then she got to do her "board" (remember the backboards you had to do for science fair projects?). I purposely saved this for last because in a way it was a type of reward. She got to draw on the board, make pictures for it, and lay it out however she wanted. I knew, though, if I had let her do this part first she never would have cooperated with the report part of the project. Having her do the project this way, I knew that she comprehended the material at every step. Feedback was an important part of the process. And to this day, Ashley can tell people the history of the Christmas tree.

The process I have described here is very similar to the system I myself use to study. It's basically a process of regurgitation, for lack of a better word. I read a chapter by first going through it and reading its topic headings. Then I go to the chapter summary and read it. By doing these two things I know what to expect or look for while I'm reading the body of the chapter. Then I go back and start reading the chapter from the beginning. After every couple of paragraphs, I stop and summarize what I've just read in my own words. If I can do this successfully, I go on reading. If I can't, I know I didn't comprehend the material and need to go back. For the best comprehension, it's a good idea to read the chapter in one sitting rather than part today and part three days later.

Using a tutor also helps to increase reading comprehension. The key is for the tutor, whether it is yourself or someone whose help you've enlisted, to make the lessons as fun or different as possible. This could entail using flash cards, reading games, or anything else that is going to amplify what your child is learning in school.

If you want to take tutoring on yourself, be prepared to put in the time and effort it requires. The best approach I have found, and one that seems to work with any subject, is a multisensory approach. For example, if your child is having difficulty with writing or spelling, you can use a teaching method that combines the use of her senses (seeing, hearing, touching, tasting, smelling). With the following suggestions, as with any work or task you introduce, start with the idea of large to small, concrete to abstract. To begin with, you can make some sandpaper letters. Trace outlines of letters or words onto sandpaper and cut them out. Then trace the letter or word with your finger and say it aloud as you trace. Have your child repeat the process. You can do something very similar to this with a salt box. Take a tray or even a lid from a shoe box and fill it with salt (sand will also work). As before, show the child how to trace letters and say them aloud. Both of these techniques use three of the five senses in combination. This is a great way for children with learning disabilities and/or dyslexia to learn, and it's adaptable for older kids, too.

Another technique to aid your child's learning is to incorporate lessons as games at any time of the day. Try playing "I Spy" at the dinner table: "I spy something that begins with a *p* sound" (pepper, plate). Baking with your child is a great way to learn fractions. Get creative; you'll be amazed at the opportunities for learning experiences in a single day.

Study Tips

Following is a list of tips and techniques that you can assist your child with in order to improve study habits and comprehension.

- *Start assignments early.* Your child has a long-term assignment, say a book report, due in six weeks. You know that it's due then because you have marked it on the calendar. Teach her the importance of getting a head start by having her work on it for fifteen minutes per night, starting six weeks beforehand and not waiting until three or four weeks before it's due like the rest of the class. In this way she only has to focus on it for fifteen minutes per night, whereas if she were to wait and start later, she would need to spend more time on it at every sitting. When this happens it is more likely she will be unable to focus and then become frustrated.

- *Write a sentence for every page.* An easy technique for book reports is to remember the rule of one sentence for every page. In other words, after the child reads a page, he writes down a one-sentence summary of what he has read. If he continues to do this for the whole book, by the time he's done he will have a report all ready.

- *Review for tests.* When studying for tests, always review the lecture notes.

- *Structure your notes.* For people with AD/HD this isn't as easy as it sounds. Besides staying focused on the lecture, the problem is figuring out what exactly to write down or take notes on. It involves integrating the following skills: sustained attention, comprehension of the material that's being presented, translating incoming information into a comprehensible format, coordinating hand-eye movements, and immediate memorization of the information presented so that it can be written down. Some rules to remember about taking notes are as follows:

  1. Make note of anything written on the board. More than likely, if it's written on the board, it's important.

  2. Make note of anything that gets repeated. If the teacher says something over and over, it's important and will probably be on a test.

  3. Make note of anything that the teacher puts extra emphasis on. If the teacher says, "This is important" or "This will be on the test," write it down.

  4. Make note of anything that appears in list, bulleted, or outline format. If it is presented in one of these formats either by the teacher or in the book, it is important information to know and remember, and will probably be on a test.

  It's also a good idea to teach your child just to use lines to separate main ideas while taking notes instead of trying to remember the structure of a formal outline. Also, show her how to use shorthand, such as the abbreviation "w/o" for without.

- *Study the bold print.* When studying textbooks or handouts, if it's in bold print or large print, remember it. It's a good idea to make up study questions or flash cards about words or meanings that are in bold print or serve as headings. This is the way a lot of tests are laid out. You can write the study questions down on index cards and make "study cards." As you review the cards, make two piles, those you know and those you don't know. This is a very helpful technique for both younger and older students. It's also a way for them to study and review on their own.

- *Use acronyms.* If the child has some type of listed information to memorize, teach him to use acronyms to help remember. For example, to remember the colors of the rainbow, in order, he might think of the nonsense name "Roy G. Bv." He can then write the acronym on the test paper and use it as a tool for remembering red, orange, yellow, green, blue, violet.

- *Make proofreading positive.* Proofreading is very challenging for a child with AD/HD because it requires a person to slow down the thinking process. It's helpful to teach the child to not wait until the end of writing a paper to start proofing it, but instead to check a certain amount of material at a time. In this way she can stay focused long enough to finish the project. Also, if you're helping the child do this, try to focus on the positive so she feels successful enough to want to change the negative. Take the following scenario, for example:

  > Johnny is learning how to make a cursive letter *c*. His homework consists of practicing his writing by filling a page with this letter. When he's finished, he asks you to help him check his work. You look at the page and think, "Oh, boy—we've got

problems." You can see only three or four correctly written letters. You now have two choices: You can take one of those red pens and mark every wrong letter with a slash. More than likely, though, if you do this, he's not going to want to practice his letters very much. Plus, his self-esteem will be pretty well shot. Or you can point out the letters he made correctly. "I like the way this one looks, and this one here, too. Oh, look at this one: You must have really spent time on that one. You know, Johnny, I bet if you took a few more minutes you could make a whole page just like these." With this type of reaction he will feel proud and capable. The challenge of making more is not overwhelming because you've already pointed out that he can do it. And his self-esteem remains intact.

- *Instead of looking for all of the mistakes, look for all of the correct words, spellings, and paragraphs.* Use positive reinforcement for all of the correct things and challenge the child to reexamine the other things and make them correct. A word of caution about positive reinforcement. It's not statements like "You're so smart"; it's statements like "I like the way you wrote this paragraph" or "That paper was a lot of hard work. I'm really proud of you."

Here's another list of general ideas and tools that can be very simple to do and yet extremely helpful for the child with AD/HD. These tools can be implemented by a parent or teacher, or both. They're so simple that they might sound gimmicky to you. Don't be put off by that, though, because they work!

- *Desk border.* This gets back to the concept of creating a psychic sphere or defining boundaries. Use colored tape or posterboard around the edges of the child's desk. That way she knows that all she needs to focus on is what's inside the border. For some children, depending on their sensitivity levels, you can use Velcro tape to do this. Rubbing their fingers on it actually helps some children to focus. By giving their fingers something to do, you get rid of the fidgets.

- *Viewing screen.* This is something I've used both at home and in the classroom and have found very helpful. It's the same concept as the desk border only shrunk down. Take a piece of posterboard about the size of a piece of paper or a textbook and cut it out like a picture frame mat. The child then uses this to view or read through. He can place it on worksheets or book pages. You can even use colored plastic in the middle for a screen effect. For children who are just learning to read, or if the size mentioned seems too big, you can make the frame smaller, the size of a few typed lines. The purpose of this is, again, to help the child focus only on what's inside the screen.

- *Graph paper, loose-leaf paper turned sideways, or folded sheets of paper.* These can be used if the child is having difficulty spacing her writing. Again, it's a way of defining boundaries. Each number or letter is placed in a box on the graph paper, between the lines on sideways loose-leaf, or in the folded box area of the paper sheet. This is also helpful for kids who have trouble with column-type problems in math.

- *Clean work area.* Have the rule of keeping everything off the desk or work area except what is needed in completing the current task.

- *Tape recorder.* This is a good way for older students to take notes from lectures. Of course, the child needs to let the teacher know about this beforehand. Also, some children benefit from books on tape. Check with the reference librarian at your local library for the names of associations that record books onto audiotape. The child with this need generally also demonstrates other types of learning disabilities, such as vision problems.

- *Ear protectors (industrial).* This is a way of shutting out external stimuli. I mention industrial because those radio earphones aren't much good at blocking things out.

- *Computers.* The more senses covered in the learning process, the more concrete the information processed will be. When a child uses a computer to write assignments he can see the work done, hear the sound of the keys as he types, and feel the keys. As I mentioned earlier, a computer is a lot like a TV in that it can maintain the child's attention. It's a great teaching aid, too, because instead of a lesson's being presented in front of the classroom with all of the external stimuli, the lesson takes place within the boundaries of the computer screen.

- *Special jobs.* Kids with AD/HD perform very well in leadership roles. It's also a way of keeping them involved in the classroom with an activity so the teacher can focus on something else.

- *Special interests.* When your child is given the opportunity to share with others something that she's interested in, it gives others the chance to get to know her better and possibly see a side of her they haven't seen before. This is a big help for the child who seems to have poor social standing.

- *Extracurricular activities.* These are great ways to use up some excess energy in a structured format and also to cultivate new interests.

- *Never let work extend beyond one day.* Unfinished work quickly snowballs and becomes overwhelming. Short assignments with immediate feedback are best; stress quality, not quantity.

- *Role modeling.* Model the type of behavior and work you want the child to exhibit. If you're unorganized, don't expect your child to be any different.

- *Adaptation.* Adapt the environment to the child—not the child to the environment. This includes lessons and assignments. Once the child has got the concept down, there's no need for repetitive work. He'll become bored with it. Focus on what he has completed, not what he has left undone.

- *Be consistent.* This speaks for itself.

- *Don't assume anything.* This also speaks for itself.

LEARNING DIFFICULTIES

Learning disabilities, learning difficulties, and poor school performance are common among children with AD/HD. According to Dr. Russell Barkley, when compared to other children, the risk for school failure is about two to three times greater among children with both AD/HD and learning disabilities and/or a history of poor school performance. This is not the result of a lack of intelligence by any means, as intelligence and AD/HD are unrelated. A lot of times it can be frustrating for parents when, after they have put their child on medication, her learning problems persist. This is because the medication only helps the child focus and attend to a task; it does not make her any smarter.

Learning disorders and learning disabilities are deficits in specific academic skills, in relation to expected levels of performance. Although the child's IQ may fall within the normal range, he has noticeable difficulty applying his intelligence and skills—thus, his academic achievement doesn't "match" his overall intelligence. Difficulties might make themselves evident in reading comprehension, spelling, math, handwriting, and language skills. Learning disabilities include things like dyslexia, perceptual handicaps, and developmental aphasia and dysphasia, to name a few. Characteristic symptoms include low frustration tolerance, unpredictable test performances; difficulties with reading, writing, and/or spelling; and problems performing math calculations.

According to Dr. Russell Barkley, about one-half of all learning disabled children have AD/HD, and one-third of kids with AD/HD have a learning disability. What this means is that kids with AD/HD often (but not always) have specific learning difficulties in addition to their AD/HD. If your child is having difficulties at school, meet with your child's teacher to share your concerns. Teachers often have similar concerns and welcome the opportunity to discuss these with parents. An evaluation by the school psychologist can either rule out a learning disability or confirm one so your child can get the right kind of help.

SCHOOLS AND THE LAW

By law, schools must provide what is called a "free and appropriate" education to all people between the ages of 3 and 21. This includes identification, educational evaluations, individual education plans, and education in the least restrictive environment possible.

Not all children with AD/HD need special services, but some kids with this disorder can't get an appropriate education without them. For these kids, AD/HD is an educational performance problem—that is, the disorder interferes with their learning. If your child has problems learning, he may be qualified for an individual plan and for special services. A medical diagnosis of AD/HD isn't enough to qualify the child for special services—the child must also be experiencing educational performance problems.

When these problems are evident, the parent, the child's teacher, or the school may request an evaluation for the child. The purpose of the evaluation is to determine whether or not the child has a disability and, if so, whether or not that disability meets the eligibility criteria for special services set forth in federal and state law. No matter who makes the request, the parent must be notified.

The evaluation process is similar to the diagnostic procedure for AD/HD because it, too, takes a team effort. An evaluation team usually includes psychologist(s), teacher(s), medical specialist(s), educational diagnostician(s), and others, depending on the needs of the individual child. The information comes from parent and teacher observations, the child's medical and behavioral history, and a comprehensive battery of tests, including tests for intelligence and achievement. The schools must provide the evaluation free of charge, and any tests must be administered by trained personnel.

IDEA and Section 504

Here's where things get tricky. If a child's AD/HD affects her educational performance or limits a major life activity, that child may be eligible to receive services under either the Individuals with Disabilities Education Act (IDEA) or Section 504 of the Rehabilitation Act of 1973 (Section 504, for short). If the child isn't eligible for services under the IDEA, she could be eligible under Section 504. (Remember, though, that not all children with AD/HD require special services, just those whose educational performance is limited by their AD/HD.)

These two laws achieve similar outcomes, but there are differences between them, including criteria for eligibility, services available, implementation procedures, and procedural safeguards for parents and/or the school district. Specifically, the IDEA is a programmatic law governing all special education services in the United States. It provides federal funding to schools to support special education and related services. Section 504 is actually not a law at all, though it is often referred to that way. It's a civil rights statute that prohibits recipients of federal funds from discriminating against anyone on the basis of disability. Because public schools (and many private schools as well) receive federal assistance, they are prohibited from discriminating against children who have a disability. If the school doesn't attempt to provide such children with "reasonable accommodations" so they can get an appropriate education, then that's discrimination. A school could lose its federal funding if discrimination of this kind is proved.

To be eligible for services under the IDEA, a child must meet the criteria for one of the categories the act identifies. These categories include serious emotional disturbance, learning disabilities, retardation, traumatic brain injury, autism, vision and hearing impairments, physical disabilities, and other health impairments. You'll notice that AD/HD is not on this list. However, a child with AD/HD is eligible for services if she meets the requirements of any of the other categories the IDEA specifies. For example, a child with AD/HD and a learning disability would qualify, whereas a child with AD/HD alone would not. AD/HD also sometimes fits under the category "other health impaired." According to a policy memorandum issued in 1991 by the Department of Education's Office of Special Education and Rehabilitative Services, if a child's AD/HD is a chronic or acute health problem resulting in limited alertness, the child may be considered disabled and therefore eligible for special education and related services.

If the child does not qualify under the IDEA, he may still be eligible to receive services under Section 504. As mentioned, Section 504 prohibits discrimination on the basis of disability. Disability is defined as any impairment that substantially limits one or more major life activities (and learning is a major life activity). If AD/HD limits a child's ability to learn, then the child is, by definition, disabled. Since all children are entitled to a free and appropriate public education, schools are required to make reasonable accommodations to ensure this takes place. Accommodations can include regular or special education and/or related services, depending upon the child's needs.

Most children with AD/HD who experience educational performance problems are eligible for special services under either the IDEA or Section 504. Usually children with more severe disabilities or whose disabilities fit neatly into a specific category receive services under the IDEA. Children whose problems are less severe or less well defined generally fall under Section 504 because of its less stringent eligibility criteria.

Both the IDEA and Section 504 require a plan of action, or a document that spells out what will be done to help the child. A plan under the IDEA is called an Individualized Education Program (or IEP). A Section 504 plan is drafted if the child meets those eligibility requirements. Parents should play an active role in preparing either type of plan.

The IEP

If your child qualifies for special education services, an IEP will be written. The IEP is a legal document that the school must follow. It is a written plan of action, detailing what steps are going to be taken as far as the instruction of the child. It must include the following:

- A statement of the child's current performance level

- A statement of annual goals or achievements and short-term objectives

- A statement of the specific educational and related services to be provided for the child (related services provided at no cost to parents include transportation, speech therapy, occupational therapy, and the like)

- The dates services will begin and the expected duration of each service

- A statement of evaluation procedures to determine whether objectives are being achieved

- A statement of the extent to which each child will be able to participate in regular educational programs

The school system is required by law to provide the services described in the IEP for the specified time. The law does not require that the school system reach the goals outlined in the IEP, only that sincere efforts be made toward achieving those goals. Once the IEP is completed, the parent or the school can request changes to it, but no changes can be made without parental approval. The IEP is reviewed each year so that any needed changes can be made.

The IDEA and Section 504 state that all children, with disabilities or not, must be educated together, provided that this is possible and appropriate in the school system. The IEP will include decisions as to the placement of the child: Some children can get by with the use of a special education resource room part of the time, in addition to their regular classroom time. Other children can't get by with this and need the help and support of a self-contained special education classroom, where they can receive individualized instruction and support from a specially trained professional. What services the child receives depend on the nature and severity of the child's difficulties.

The 504 Plan

Many children with AD/HD who have educational performance problems don't fit the IDEA criteria and don't qualify for special education services under this law. These children still require carefully planned and executed interventions—and they are still eligible to receive classroom accommodations and other special services under Section 504. The 504 plan is less formal than the IEP and therefore may be a quicker way to go and involve less bureaucratic red tape. Because it is less formal, though, there are fewer legal safeguards for parents. Like the IEP, the 504 plan documents the child's needs and spells out ways the school will attempt to meet them—for example, a child might receive the services of the school social worker, have an individualized disciplinary plan, or have specific accommodations in the classroom. Often the success of these children hinges on their teachers' willingness and ability to adapt the classroom environment to meet their needs.

According to a 1991 memorandum by the Department of Education, some of these accommodations include the following:

- A structured learning environment

- Repeating and simplifying instructions about in-class and homework assignments

- Supplementing verbal instructions with visual instructions

- Using behavioral management techniques

- Adjusting class schedules

- Modifying test delivery

- Using tape recorders, computer-aided instruction, and other audiovisual equipment

- Selecting modified textbooks and workbooks

- Individualizing homework assignments

Other provisions range from consultation to special resources and may include reducing class size; use of one-on-one tutorials; classroom aides and note takers; involvement of a services coordinator to oversee implementation of special programs and services; and possible modification of nonacademic times such as lunchroom, recess, and physical education.

If You Disagree . . .

Despite the protections guaranteed by the IDEA and Section 504, many children with AD/HD continue to be denied access to an appropriate range of special education and/or related services. Myths and ignorance about AD/HD unfortunately continue, even though scientific research has documented AD/HD as a neurobiological disability. Children with AD/HD who do not exhibit behavior problems often get lost in the shuffle of the classroom and in administrative red tape because their disabilities don't stand out. The result can be a one-way ticket to frustration, low self-esteem, academic failure, and emotional difficulties.

If you think your child's AD/HD is causing educational problems but the evaluation team believes your child isn't eligible for services under either the IDEA or Section 504, you don't have to let the matter drop there. As mentioned earlier, you have the right to request an evaluation of your child at any time. You also have the right to appeal the conclusions of the evaluation, and the school is required to provide you with information about appeal procedures.

It's very important to keep careful records. In those records include your observations, teachers' observations, and a record of communications between home and school. It's a good idea to make copies of any letters sent to the school. This information will be useful even if you and your child's school do agree about services for your child, and it's essential if you and the school disagree. Remember that parents and their children are guaranteed certain rights under federal and state laws. The process for ensuring these rights, however, can be confusing and intimidating. Check with your child's school about a parent advocate service in your community. It may also be necessary to retain an attorney if you decide to appeal a decision; it is very likely that the school district will have its own legal counsel in such an appeal.

Parents should be and, by law, must be included in all of these processes. As your child's advocate, you will need to familiarize yourself with the details of the IDEA and Section 504 of the Rehabilitation Act. For more detailed information, I suggest reading *Attention Deficit Disorder and the Law: A Guide for Advocates,* listed at the end of this book.

Something for you to remember, though, is that just because these laws exist does not mean that your child's needs will automatically be addressed. More and more, funding for special education and other programs is being cut back. AD/HD is "invisible," so it often gets overlooked. Realize, too, that these laws intend for states to meet only minimum requirements. They do not require schools to guarantee a child will reach his fullest potential. In accordance with the 14th Amendment, the school system has to provide a free and appropriate public education—this is the base for you to work from.

WEAKNESSES OR STRENGTHS?

It's important to remember that children with AD/HD do have strengths that can enhance learning and living and add to the life of the classroom and home. For each difficulty a child may have, there is frequently a flip side. With distractibility often comes creativity and ingenuity; impulsivity is often accompanied by spontaneity and enthusiasm. These children can bring humor, originality, and sensitivity to their world. The proactive teacher or parent values and nurtures these strengths and regards them as assets to the learning and living process.

Chapter 7

Stop, Look, and Listen: What to Do about Misbehavior

$\mathcal{A}$ll children at times choose to behave ineffectively. In other words, they misbehave. Kids with AD/HD are no different.

Through your observations and knowledge of your child, you have probably been able to identify—and, I hope, address—many of the external causes of your child's misbehavior, such as environmental factors, boundary issues, or problems with transitions.

External causes of misbehavior are easier to detect than internal causes. These internal causes usually concern unmet needs, especially the desire to feel powerful. Even though internal needs are sometimes difficult to understand, it's important for you to look for them when you attempt to change your child's behavior. Getting a grip on your child's misbehavior also means making a commitment to deal constructively with conflict and to understand and use basic behavior management principles. In this chapter I want to look at all these things.

UNMET NEEDS AND POWER STRUGGLES

Oftentimes, kids feel it's unsafe to express their needs because it doesn't pay off for them. How many times as parents have we heard the phrase "I'm bored" and responded with "Well, go do something then!" If you think about it, that response really makes no sense at all. If the child had something to do, he wouldn't be bored, would he? Or we respond, "What do you mean, bored? Wish

I had time to be bored!" Nothing like laying down some guilt and shame. You are saying, in other words, how could you be bored if I'm not bored? Personally, I think the tendency to induce guilt and shame is a genetically determined trait that kicks in when you become a parent. The problem with guilt and shame is that they aren't very effective tools in parenting. First, we have to make it safe for children to express their needs. This means leaving guilt and shame out of the picture. Next we have to be willing to listen to those needs. If we do this, we alter our children's pattern of choosing misbehavior to get their needs met. The key is to show children ways to assert themselves effectively and safely, to make their voices heard.

Let's look at this need to feel powerful a little more closely. Everyone has this need, but because children have few legitimate ways of expressing it, they often try to meet this need in other ways. When their attempts fail, misbehavior is usually the result. And this often takes the form of a power struggle. We as parents need to ask ourselves, "What kind of power is my child seeking to increase, and in what legitimate way can my child ask to receive that power?" Children do have the right to feel powerful. Can you imagine being denied that right, even as a child? More than likely you'd be incapable of thinking, feeling, or doing anything without somebody's first telling you to do it. Letting your child express a need for power legitimately doesn't mean you let your child take away your power as a parent and run your life. It simply means offering her a voice and a choice in her own life. It's about giving her some say in the matter and letting her know it counts.

Oftentimes we as parents think we have to be right (this appears to be another predetermined pattern in parenting). What happens, though, is that we are choosing being right over having a closer relationship with the other person. In the following scenario, it's Johnny's chore to feed the dog. Mom sees that this hasn't been done yet, and being the logical person she is, she wants to make sure Johnny takes care of it. If he doesn't, she believes it will give Johnny the message that he can get away with not doing his chores.

Mom: Johnny, you need to feed the dog now.

Johnny: I'm busy. I'll do it later.

Mom: I said to do it now. (Thinking, "No, he won't—he'll forget and then I'll have to. He won't learn responsibility that way.")

Johnny: And I said I would—later! (Thinking, "Why doesn't she ever listen to me—doesn't she believe me?")

Mom: (Very threatening tone, getting Mom nowhere) Do it now or else . . . You know I feel so sorry for that dog, always having to wait on you for food! (Nothing like using a little guilt and shame for a motivator.)

Johnny: FINE! ("Sure, she feels sorry for the dog—she doesn't care how I feel.")

This is an example of a typical power struggle. Sure, the task finally gets done, but not without a lot of anger and hurt feelings first. Now let's take another look at this situation. It's the same scenario, but Mom is being proactive this time. When Johnny is in a symptom-controlled state, calm and collected, she approaches him.

Mom: Johnny, I see it's your job to feed the dog this week. Would you like to do that at 5:00 or 6:00?

Johnny: I guess 6:00.

Mom: So what is it you're going to do at 6:00?

Johnny: Feed the dog.

Mom: (It's now 6:00.) Johnny, it's 6:00. (She touches his shoulder, makes direct eye

contact, remains calm, and smiles.)
Do you remember what you chose to
do now? (She maintains this calm
demeanor, staying right in front of him.)

Johnny: Yeah, but I'm busy. (Sees she's not
going to leave.)

Mom: (Keeps smiling calmly and begins to
guide him toward the dog food.) It's
6:00. So how was football practice?
(Changing the subject as they get closer
to the dog food)

When you give a child a voice and a choice you legitimize his need for power and eliminate his need for a power struggle. Your part in this is to be unwilling to engage in a power struggle—and if you've clearly defined the situation and given choices that you can live with, you won't need to. Again, it helps to have prestanding agreements—made when the child is in a symptom-controlled state.

Another form of power struggle, taken to the extreme, is the temper tantrum. Temper tantrums are the only behavior that you ignore, or don't take part in at all. You do have to set limits effectively and proactively, however. If a child chooses to have a temper tantrum, that's fine; it's her choice. More than likely she doesn't realize she's choosing this behavior, so it's up to you to help her come to that realization. I'll discuss a way to do this without getting into a power struggle later in this chapter.

RESOLVING CONFLICT

Conflict is a part of life—between adults and between adults and children. The goal is not to eliminate conflict altogether (that would be impossible). Rather, what we need to do as parents is to deal with our inevitable conflicts with our children openly, directly, and fairly. One way we can do this is through *successful confrontation*. I discussed successful confrontation earlier, in chapter 3, as it relates to sibling conflicts, but the approach also works with adults and children (and also with adults and adults). Most misbehavior will decrease after successful confrontation. The steps in successful confrontation are as follows:

1. State the problem.

2. State your want/need.

3. State how you'll support the child in this.

The following example shows how this works: Tyrell, age 15, has stayed out past his 10:00 curfew. Mom says, "It's a half hour past your curfew. I want to talk to you about this, and I know you want a chance to explain. Right now I'm really angry though, so we should wait until morning to talk. Does that work for you? . . . Thanks. Good night."

In order for it to be effective, confrontation should be a two-way learning process. You are learning what the child needs and wants, and what the goals of his misbehavior are. He in turn is learning from you better methods of decision making and problem solving so that next time he will circumvent the behavior and choose a better route. Do the intervention immediately, as soon as you are aware that the behavior is taking place. Next give everyone involved a chance to cool off. After that, you can initiate a conversation about the problematic behavior.

Basically, you will need to explain how the child's behavior affects and hurts others and what its impact is. Then ask him what he can do differently. You need to explain what's wrong with a behavior, what a better choice would be, and why that choice would be better (that is, because it leads to a win-win situation). You may need to "sell" the child on why it would be better to handle the situation in a different way and then redirect him to another activity.

When you're doing all this, it's important to remember not to give a lecture or lesson about how things were a lot different when you were younger. When you get on a soapbox, you're unapproachable and unable then to see eye-to-eye with the child. This is also your opportunity to listen carefully to the child to get more information about what the child's real needs are in the situation.

After your child misbehaves, allow her to correct the misbehavior as soon as possible. This can be done in at least three ways, including apologizing, making amends, or making repayment. An apology can be either written or verbal. You can offer your support in this if it's needed. Sometimes I feel it is even better to make amends. When you apologize to someone, that's all it really is, an apology. Making amends involves a little bit more because you also offer to fix the situation by doing things differently from now on. It's a way of following through and making up for any inconvenience caused by the misbehavior. It's not about trying to undo what's already been done; rather, it's about improving things for the future. Repayment follows along these same lines, whether it is done with money, physical work, or time. Repayment with time, for example, might involve saying to a child, "Your delay cost me about 10 minutes of my time. You will need to help me for 10 minutes with my chores tonight."

Another direct way to resolve conflicts involves *brainstorming*. Brainstorming is a way of negotiating and solving problems so all can get their needs met. It involves the following eight steps:

1. Ask the person you're in conflict with for permission to work out the problem.

2. State the problem as simply and clearly as possible, with no guilt, shame, or blame.

3. Share how you feel with "I" statements. For example, "I felt really disappointed when I saw the dishes hadn't been done," not "You never remember to do the dishes."

4. Ask the other person to share how she feels and what she wants.

5. Write down a list of possible solutions—don't be negative or reject any ideas.

6. Give the other person the list and have her cross out any ideas that make her unhappy; then you do the same.

7. Pick one of the ideas or a combination of the suggestions that are not crossed out to which you can both agree; don't agree to anything that you are unhappy with or resentful about. Everyone has veto power.

8. Use the agreed-upon solution for an agreed-upon time period; if it doesn't work out, start the process over.

Brainstorming can be used in a variety of situations, not just when there is a conflict—from negotiating chores to drawing up a behavior contract to help reduce an unacceptable behavior.

WHAT IS BEHAVIOR MANAGEMENT?

Behavior management means strengthening behavior through positive reinforcement and weakening or lessening behavior through natural or logical consequences. Reinforcements or consequences that are enjoyable will strengthen a behavior so that it's likely to occur again. When there's no reinforcement or payoff, the behavior becomes weaker and eventually stops altogether. It's a lot like putting money into a candy machine; if you stop getting candy, you stop putting money into the machine. Reinforcements and consequences don't have to be dramatic; their power lies in the message they send to the person who receives them.

I choose to use the term *reinforcement* rather than *reward*. I do this because some people feel that rewarding a child for good behavior is bribery. I don't condone bribery. Reinforcement is a way of conveying positive information or giving feedback, whereas rewards tend to be material objects and reinforce only materialism. You should not feel the need to buy your child a toy every time he does something good. You should, however, feel the need to relay information that lets him know whether his behavior is acceptable or unacceptable. Your child should be able to feel a positive result from positive behavior and also feel (though not physically) a negative result from negative behavior.

Punishment

I'd like to address the subject of punishment so that we might get this useless tool—really it's a weapon—out of the way. Behavior management is accomplished by positive reinforcement. Some people don't accept this because there is no immediate solution to the problem behavior. That's why punishment is so attractive— it seems to offer an immediate answer. It doesn't. In fact, it just creates a bigger problem by damaging the child's emotional well-being. But because we can't see this damage, we think the problem is solved. Punishment is an immediate response, but it's the parent's immediate response, not the child's. It serves as a form of venting for the parent. By displaying our superiority and ultimate control, we vent our discontent with the present situation. Maybe the child does stop the misbehavior, so it must have worked, right? Wrong. The child stopped because she was motivated by fear, not necessarily of physical harm, but rather fear of things getting worse: "I'd better stop it 'cause I'm bad" or "Wow, they're really mad. If I don't stop they're likely to lose it and I'll be in even more trouble!" Using fear as the main motivator to change behavior is not healthy—in the long run, when the child doesn't have anyone standing over her to be afraid of, it's going to result in severe consequences. She'll reason, "I must be doing OK because I haven't got caught yet (or nobody's yelling at me yet)." She won't have learned to redirect her behavior and make a more effective choice. Instead, she will have learned that unless someone reprimands her, she must be doing OK.

Punishment conveys limited and often incorrect information. It tells your child only what he shouldn't do. He will more than likely just find another equally unacceptable activity to keep himself occupied. Punishment often results in a power struggle where both parent and child are backed into corners and no one comes out winning. It often backfires, leading to increased undesirable behavior. And it often means spanking. Spanking a child with AD/HD is a futile effort that may even lead to child abuse.

So you should rely only on positive consequences, right? Wrong. That would be unrealistic—positive consequences alone are not enough. The first thing we as parents need to do is to eliminate the word *punishment* from our vocabulary and give up our roles as wardens and dictators. We need to take back our role as teachers and instead use the terms *natural consequence* or *logical consequence*. When using natural consequences or logical consequences, the point is to guide the child away from the misbehavior and not to shame, hurt, or humiliate. Before looking at these types of consequences, I want first to stress the importance of positive reinforcement.

Positive Reinforcement

Positive reinforcement, also known as positive consequences, is probably the most powerful and constructive tool in behavior management. Choosing positive reinforcements carefully will determine the success of your behavior management program. They need to be meaningful to your child. So think about what activities and privileges your child values and enjoys the most. The simpler the positive reinforcement, the better. Activities that your child now takes for granted can be incorporated as positive reinforcements: a Saturday morning bike trip, a day without chores, a trip to the park, staying up an extra half hour. Using them successfully depends a great deal on how you present them—for example, "You can't go outside until you finish your chores" is not as effective as "When you finish your chores you may go out and play."

Timing is crucial in using positive reinforcement. Any type of reinforcement or consequence is only going to be effective when it immediately follows the behavior. Kids with AD/HD want and need immediate reinforcement; when there is a delay it can become confusing to them, and the behavior you want to see more of will likely take longer to develop. Positive reinforcement needs to occur often. Studies of children with AD/HD show that when reinforcements are few and far between their behavior tends to deteriorate.

Throughout this book, I have mentioned the importance of breaking tasks into steps. It's also important to use positive reinforcement after each step. A child with AD/HD will not want to continue working toward a goal unless she feels the success of completing each step of the process. A huge reward isn't going to mean much if she has to encounter a huge amount of frustration to obtain it. Positive reinforcement serves as a sort of gauge for the child with AD/HD to measure her success. When she receives the reinforcement, she feels the desire and motivation to continue learning and take another step toward her goal. It is also very important not to offer positive reinforcements until after the behavior has occurred. It's a lot like the old saying "Don't count your chickens until they're hatched."

Parents need to be very careful to avoid the "goodies" trap; relying on rewards such as toys and treats is materialistic, unrealistic, and expensive. Unless it is something you would ordinarily purchase for the child after he has "earned" it, it's useless to buy things that soon lose their meaning and value to the child. A less materialistic approach is to allow the child the privilege of "renting" the object. In this way the child rents a privilege (for example, using the stereo or Nintendo) on a week-to-week basis for as long as his behavior warrants. If the behavior becomes unacceptable, then he loses his renting privileges until it becomes acceptable again.

Try your best to vary positive reinforcements. Children with AD/HD become bored much easier than other children, and by varying the reinforcements you can keep their interest. It's important to use lots of positive feedback. As parents of children with AD/HD we share the common tendency to rely on criticism. For us this is natural because in the past it was at times the only way we could get a response from the child. We need to stop doing this—it doesn't work over the long run. Positive feedback doesn't cost a cent, is very easy to use, and can be delivered immediately. Another reinforcement is allowing your child to catch you telling someone else about her good behavior. And when you do this be precise in your statement—"Ashley made her bed today without being reminded" is much clearer than "Ashley's been so good lately." For some kids, accepting praise can be a new and uncomfortable experience. In this case you can praise the task done rather than the child until she becomes comfortable with this new feeling.

Logical and Natural Consequences

A logical consequence is a consequence that is a result of a behavior or that is related to the behavior. Basically it's the action of removing a privilege. For example, when Susie leaves her bike out at night, the logical consequence is that she loses the privilege of riding her bike for the next day or two. If you say that because Susie leaves her bike out she doesn't get to watch TV the next day, there's no direct relationship between the action and the privilege. The key with this tool is to remove the privilege only for a short time; otherwise it becomes ineffective because the child assumes the attitude "Oh, well, I've already lost everything anyway."

Natural consequences are the natural sequence of events that follows the misbehavior. They are spontaneous lessons on life and can send powerful messages. With natural consequences you don't need to intervene. Be patient, quiet, and detached from the situation, and allow the natural chain of events to occur. Natural consequences are things like feeling sick after you overeat or getting wet after insisting that it isn't important to wear a raincoat. In the previous example of Susie's bike being left out all night, the natural consequence to that would be that the bicycle chain gets rusty because it rained. Even though natural consequences can be a powerful learning tool, they are not always the most efficient or safest way to learn a lesson. They may not result in an immediate consequence, or they may jeopardize the child's health; you need to weigh the pluses and minuses in deciding whether or not to use a natural consequence.

Time-out is a good example of a logical consequence. The standard version of time-out involves having the child sit in a chair or another out-of-the-way spot for a certain amount of time. My version of time-out is a little different. The simple fact is that you can't make a hyperactive child sit still in a chair for five minutes—it doesn't work! My version, *quieting time,* is designed to help the child calm down and focus his attention on whatever action is appropriate or should be taking place. At either a family meeting or a time when the child is attentive to what you're saying, you need to explain what quieting time is like. For example, you might say, "I've noticed that I've been nagging and yelling at you a lot, and I don't like doing that. Instead I would like to do something called quieting time." Then continue on to explain what it is. Everyone in the home should choose a quiet place, a place where it's known they should not be disturbed. Yes, that's right—everyone. One of the best ways to teach your child what to do when he is angry or stressed out or needs to get a grip on his behavior is for you to model it for him. And it's good for you, too!

You also need to explain to your child the consequences if she chooses not to go to her place for quieting time when she is asked to. The goal is for the child to recognize unacceptable behavior and understand what she can do for herself to head off that behavior. Quieting time can be used for any inappropriate behavior— hitting, yelling, speaking disrespectfully, and so forth.

Quieting time is also a good response when you and your child are locked in the all-out power struggle of a temper tantrum. First, you will need to discuss the behavior with the child when he is, again, in a symptom-controlled state. If he doesn't already have a designated quieting place, he needs to choose one now. Explain what will happen if he chooses to have a temper tantrum: "If you choose to have a temper tantrum you will need to go to your room until you are calm. Temper tantrums are your choice, and I'm not willing to be part of them." Next, tell him, "You can choose to go to your room on your own, or I will walk you there. If you don't choose to go to your room, that tells me to choose for you."

When your child does have a temper tantrum, your job is simply to follow through with the prestanding agreement. State calmly, "I see that you're choosing to have a temper tantrum. I'm not willing to be part of it. You need to go calm down. Are you going on your own, or do you need me to walk you there?" If he ignores you, say, "This tells me I need to choose for you," and guide him to his room. When you are speaking to him you need to remain calm, using a firm but gentle tone. State things clearly and simply—don't lecture. After you have gently guided him to his quiet-time spot, state, "When you choose to be calm you may come back and we'll talk." If your child is really defiant, you may need to take him to quiet time several times. Continue to do this until he stays in quiet time—that may take twenty to thirty tries at first, but be willing to be consistent and persistent in order to establish this boundary.

Remember, too, that a child who has AD/HD may not know what calm is. You actually have to identify it for her. But how do you do that when she's in the middle of a fit? The second that she stops or pauses, even if it's just to take a breath, you need to jump right in and say, "That's calm! You're calm." With young children this is kind of easy. It's the moment when, after screaming and crying at the top of their lungs, they make one of those muffled gasps for air just before they let out their next scream. That's the moment you jump in. At first they look at you like you're crazy and begin to scream again. At that point you state, "Oh, no, I'm sorry, that's not calm. When you're calm you can come out." And then they realize, "Hey, wait a minute. I almost got out of this; she said I was calm, but now I'm not. OK, what was I doing when she said that; oh, I stopped screaming; that must be calm." And they proceed to calm down.

One of the advantages of this approach is that it travels. Just choose a quieting spot wherever you might be. If you're within walking distance of your car, use the car for the quieting spot. You will need to be proactive in preparing the child and clearly define what will happen if he chooses to have a temper tantrum while you are in this particular place. If he chooses to have one, follow through. Leave whatever you're doing, walk him to the car, and place him inside of it (with the window open a crack, please). You are to stand on the outside with your back to him. Do not get inside—otherwise you will be taking part in his tantrum. Remind him that he needs to get calm. When he does finally choose this, let him know that you're glad he made this choice. In this way you are reinforcing the fact that he can choose his behavior.

Whether you choose time-out (the old version) or quieting time, you need to be consistent with it and label it positively as an opportunity for the child to calm down and think about what just happened and what she could have chosen to do differently. For example, "You bad girl! Now you have to go to time-out" is ineffective. Instead, say, "Hitting is unacceptable. You will need to go to time-out and think about what just happened and what you will do differently next time."

Behavior Contracts

A behavior contract is a way to help your child improve a particular problem behavior. Using the techniques of successful confrontation, you first discuss the target behavior with the child. Next you brainstorm a desired replacement behavior. Finally, you include consequences and reinforcements, write the agreement down, and have both parties sign it. A contract can be quite simple, as the following example shows.

4-15-98

I agree to have my chores done every day by 6:00 without being reminded by Mom or Dad. For each day I achieve this, I will earn a dollar in addition to my usual allowance. For each day I do not achieve this, I agree to pay Mom and Dad a dollar reminder fee.

Matt

Mom/Dad

MISBEHAVIOR DO'S AND DON'TS

To sum up, here are some things you *don't* want to do when you respond to your child's misbehavior:

- Ignore the misbehavior: Unfortunately, pretending the behavior is not there will not make it go away. The only exception to this rule is when your child is having a temper tantrum.

- Nag: When you nag someone you might as well be saying, "Please ignore 80 percent of everything I've said." When you nag, people learn to tune you out. It doesn't work—stop it.

- Use the word "OK" following a statement: For example, "You may not use your bike for the rest of the day, OK?" You're probably saying this to make sure you made yourself clear, but the child interprets it as "Is it all right that I take your bike away?"

- Wait to step in until both you and your child have lost it: You may feel that if you were to intervene every time something happened you'd be stepping in constantly, but the fact is if you intervene early you will reduce the number of times you need to intervene over the long run.

- Yell and scream: You can't control anyone else's behavior until you are in control of your own.

And here are some things you *do* want to remember to do:

- Focus on one problem at a time until you see some substantial progress, and then move on to the next problem.

- Talk about the problem using "I" statements rather than "you" statements. That is, say, "I'm unwilling to prepare different meals for everyone" instead of "You need to eat your dinner because it's good for you."

- Focus on what you can do to make the situation different.

- Set limits to convey the message of self-respect.

- Remember that children don't have to suffer to learn.

Chapter 8

Creating Powerful People

*I*n order to work effectively with AD/HD, we need to help our children feel successful, and one way to do this is by building up their self-esteem. We do this by replacing the negatives with positives, focusing on strengths, and working with weaknesses. We create opportunities for success. Increasing our children's sense of self-esteem will enable them to develop a greater sense of personal power.

ENCOURAGEMENT

Encouragement is probably the most beneficial tool to work with to build a child's self-esteem. It stimulates a person to become more aware of her capabilities and of her sense of self-worth. When a child learns to feel good about herself, she's developing positive self-esteem, with the ultimate goal being the ability to apply encouragement to herself. The goal is to get her to a place where she can rely on healthy self-talk to encourage herself, rather than hearing it only from an outside source. Encouragement is food for the soul—a steady diet of it over a long period of time strengthens the child's self-esteem and also prevents the sense of self from crumbling under stress.

Encouragement manifests itself in your underlying attitude— your opinions, level of trust, tone of voice, actions, and words. What you need to remember, though, is to avoid giving the child compliments that he then feels he has to live up to, like "You are so smart!" or "You look so nice!" This is not encouragement, but rather false praise. Instead use comments that go straight to the point, like "I really like the way you handled that. It was a challenge, and you stuck with it—that's great!" or "You have a wonderful sense of fashion!"

When you first start doing this with a child, you may have to backtrack even further and compliment the finished product rather than the child's action. For example, after a child sweeps the floor you might respond, "Wow, this floor looks great!" This is the child who is so used to frustration that her self-esteem is very low and she isn't ready to admit to herself yet that she is capable of doing something right or that she is deserving of encouragement. But she is comfortable with this form of indirect encouragement. From here we can build up to "Hey, you did a fantastic job sweeping this floor!"

A suggestion made earlier and worth repeating here is to let your child catch you talking about him in an encouraging way. In other words, let him overhear a conversation you're having with someone about how proud you are of his effort to finish his chores or how you like the way he's been working at getting his homework handed in on time. This is another great form of indirect encouragement that lets him know that this isn't just some act, that you really do care and want to share that with others.

ESTABLISHING AN ENCOURAGING ATMOSPHERE

There are several tools you can use to establish an encouraging atmosphere in your family. Start by talking *with* your child instead of talking *to* her. Touch her gently, get eye contact, and use short, simple words and verbal feedback. Talking to her gives her no choice. It's one-way communication—yours. It only teaches the child to keep her thoughts and feelings to herself, which is very discouraging for her. Talking with someone means that a two-way learning process is going on. It shows respect for the person's uniqueness. You discover her logic, opinions, and point of view, and she gets credit for her creativity—this is encouraging.

Teach your child that life is a process of making choices. He needs to realize that he can assert himself through effective decision making. Sometimes children with AD/HD depend on others to make choices for them, or they just do things without realizing they have choices in the matter. Take advantage of opportune moments to ask, "What do you think you could do now?" This reminds the child of his ability to take action to make things different. It also gives him a sense of his impact on the world.

It's best if you're able to adjust your help—in other words, give your child assistance without becoming overinvolved. In this way, she can feel her strengths with the knowledge that you're there to support her. This sends the message of your faith in her abilities. Too much help doesn't convey this message. Help her out only during part of an activity—the beginning, middle, or end—but not during all of it. Remember that help should be supportive; it should be offered but not forced. For example, you might say, "You know where to find me if you need me" or "Do the best you can for five minutes, and then I'll come check on you."

Along these lines adopt a "You can do it!" philosophy that shows faith in your child's ability. Give him legitimate decision-making power, and he will have a sense of being more in charge of his life. This takes trust on your part, though. I think, as parents, this is probably one of the hardest things to do. We don't want to see our children hurt or negatively affected in any way, and we feel it's our responsibility to ensure their safety and happiness. Trusting them means letting go of some of this responsibility. We must allow them to take on challenging tasks if we expect them to grow.

This is not to say, though, that you should go to the other extreme. When obstacles face your child, you need to be able to give reassurance. Your job is to give him supportive reminders to either start or continue a task. For example, "All beginnings are difficult" or "This looks like quite a challenge; it will be fun to see how it turns out!" Realize, too, that he probably has some very realistic concerns about his own ability. Try to understand these concerns and feelings, and express this understanding sincerely to your child. This is comforting to him and enables him to get unstuck.

Parents need to emphasize the child's gains, instead of focusing on weaknesses. You can do this by pointing out that her current level of performance is an improvement on past performances. For example, "Hey, it's getting easier for you, isn't it?" or "You know, I can remember when doing this was really scary for you, and now you really enjoy it." Remember to break tasks into small, manageable steps so that she can cope with one thing at a time, and be ready to admire her progress after each step. Even a small gain is a gain to be satisfied about. Self-confidence can't be built by focusing on weaknesses. When pointing out these gains, comment on the completion of the task mastered rather than the quality of the work. Don't worry, this will come soon enough. What's important here is the amount of effort that went into completing the task and the degree of enjoyment in the process. It's process, not product, that's important. Don't get me wrong, quality is desirable. But if you're not careful, placing too much emphasis on quality could lead to perfectionism. Making mistakes is a natural part of the learning process. View them as opportunities to learn.

Let your child know that he's not alone. A great many people have been affected with this disorder and have done very well, thank you. Some of them have even used their symptomatic behaviors to their advantage. Also, a great many people are currently affected with this disorder. It may come as a surprise to both you and your child that more than likely others in his circle of friends are also affected with AD/HD. Encourage him to identify with others who share his challenge by joining the local ChADD group (many sponsor groups just for kids) or by subscribing to the newsletter *Putting on the Brakes*. (These resources are listed at the back of this book.)

Encouragement is a great tool to utilize with this child or any child; even adults benefit from it. It's free, and you can use it wherever you are and whenever you have an opportunity.

PERSONAL POWER

There are two kinds of power: role power and personal power. Role power is based on an external source. It's power that someone enjoys because of a particular role in life—for instance, parents, teachers, law enforcement officers, and judges. Personal power is based on an inner source. It's something you get because you want it and you work for it. Role power depends on wielding power over others; it may be something a person desires but will never have because only some people can have it. Personal power is different in that it has nothing to do with others, only you. You can have it immediately, and you can have as much of it as you want—and, most important, anyone can have it. There will always be someone who has role power over us; this is a fact of life. Our energies are much better spent in developing our own personal power rather than fighting the role power of others. This doesn't mean we have to agree with other people's role power, but rather that we must accept its existence and make decisions as to whether or not that power will have an impact on our lives. You do this by paying attention to your feelings and making choices. When you have choices you have power. And when you make your choices and follow through with them, this is called "having integrity."

Quite simply, personal power means to be secure and confident in oneself. It is the ultimate sense of power because it comes from within. It has four parts: being responsible, making choices, getting to know yourself, and getting and using power in your relationships and your life. All these things are important for anyone to have, but they are crucial for children with AD/HD because these children grow up to be adults with AD/HD. If a child doesn't learn to implement personal power in her life early on, it's likely adulthood will present many unnecessary challenges for her, and some of those challenges will be life altering, not only for her but for all who are close to her. I don't mean to discourage you with a forecast of gloom and doom. On the contrary, my goal is for you as parents to realize that you can make a difference in your child's life.

Teaching children with AD/HD the first part of this equation, being responsible, can be tricky. Being responsible means being accountable for your behavior and feelings. You are responsible for the kind of person you are and how you live your life. Because children with AD/HD aren't aware of much of their behavior and its effects on themselves and others, teaching them responsibility poses a challenge. The first step is to make them aware of their behavior and its impact on their place in life and on others around them. "They made me do it" is a common response for these children. We need to teach them that no one can make you do anything; you always have choices. No one can talk you into something unless you actually choose to do it. Children with AD/HD do not readily see this, though, and parents need to help. In teaching responsibility, it's also important to show children that they are not responsible for others' behaviors and that being responsible does not mean being perfect.

The second part of instilling personal power—teaching children to make choices—is paramount for children with AD/HD. They need to know that making choices is at the heart of being responsible. They need to be shown that actions are tied to feelings. Too often these children feel or are made to feel that they don't have choices in life, that bad things naturally just keep happening to them. They don't understand the concept of choosing how they react to life's problems. Our job, then, is to teach them the difference between effective and ineffective choices and show them how to make educated choices. Making an educated choice means deciding what to expect as a result of the choice and knowing whether or not that expectation is realistic. That is, what do we hope will happen and what are the chances that it will happen? In making choices it's important to remember that we can't control how others behave or feel.

The third part of personal power is teaching children to get to know themselves. Sound silly? It's not. Children with AD/HD are so used to judging and labeling themselves based on the opinions and reactions of others that they sometimes don't know how to think or feel for themselves. To help them, parents need to teach them the right names for the feelings they are having. When you know the name of a feeling it allows you to make a choice in choosing and using it. Feelings aren't facts, and they're not right or wrong; they just are. Encourage your child to find someone to talk to about his feelings and help him understand that all feelings are OK to have. Let him know how special his feelings are, that they are gifts no one can take from him or change unless he allows that to happen.

The fourth part of instilling personal power is showing children just how powerful they are. You can help them feel personally powerful by standing up for themselves—for example, by teaching them how to say, "I won't talk to you that way. Please don't talk to me that way" or "I have something to say that I think is important. Would you please listen?" This might sound crazy to parents who are dealing with defiance and power struggles on a daily basis. There is a difference, though. A child (or an adult for that matter) who knows her own personal power doesn't feel the need for power struggles. You can also point out your child's personal power when she uses her own abilities to achieve a goal: "All that studying really paid off. You did it—no one else."

If the concept of personal power is new to you, all of the preceding may seem pretty unrealistic. You're probably waiting for me to end with "and they all lived happily ever after." Well, stop waiting because I'm not going to tell you that. This is not a fairy tale. The fact is that everyone on this earth is responsible for his own happiness. No one else can make you happy, nor does your happiness depend on anyone else's behavior. Your happiness depends on one thing alone—YOU. Life is full of challenges, both good and bad. You have control over how you will react to those challenges and whether they will have a positive or a negative effect on your life.

Kids need to know what powerful people they are. They can be responsible for their behavior and feelings, and they can make choices about those behaviors and feelings. They can name and claim their feelings, future dreams, and their needs. They can have power in their relationships with others, and they can take charge of their own lives.

AD/HD IN ADULTS

The standard response when someone found out a child had AD/HD used to be "Don't worry. He'll outgrow it." Research now shows us that this is not true. AD/HD is not outgrown. The symptoms don't disappear; they simply take on a different form. I don't tell you this to depress you, further frustrate you, or take away your hopes. I say it so that you can adapt and dispense with any unrealistic expectations. It's unrealistic to say, "He'll grow out of it, and things will be better then." He has a disorder that he will have for the rest of his life. That's being realistic. But he already has a great advantage: He has you for a parent. You obviously want to make a difference, or you wouldn't be reading this book.

There are two paths individuals with this disorder can take in life. They either use the disorder to their advantage, coping and compensating in adulthood, or they continue on the path of frustration and have a very difficult time of it. For the most part, untreated adults have many, many problems in life.

One can work with AD/HD at any age. It's great if it is recognized and worked with early in life, but the old saying "It's never too late" is also true. For adults just starting to treat their AD/HD, this means getting rid of the old habits and behaviors and structuring and implementing new ones. Adults do this for themselves in the same ways parents do this for their children:

- Planning ahead

- Structuring transitions

- Creating and working out schedules

- Establishing boundaries

- Asking for help

- Networking

- Practicing stress reduction

- Incorporating organization

- Practicing effective communication

When you are parenting children who will grow up to be adults with AD/HD, it's a good idea to keep in mind the "hundred-foot rule." Don't worry about anything more than a hundred feet or a hundred days ahead of you. Take care of what needs to be done today, and tomorrow will take care of itself. Kids with AD/HD do grow up, and many are indistinguishable from their peers. As with anyone entering adulthood, some have trouble adapting to the increased responsibilities. Don't worry! Many adults with AD/HD are gainfully employed and self-supporting. However, frequently these adults have low self-esteem or a poor self-concept. However, this can be alleviated through early diagnosis and combined interventions over a period of years. Children with AD/HD whose multimodal treatment is long-term and directed toward individual symptoms of the disorder have more positive outcomes.

The insights of adults with AD/HD whose treatment has been approached in this way are giving us clues to the things that helped them, or would have helped them, the most. These include having a mentor in their lives—someone who listened to them and talked to them; having someone able to explain the various aspects of their disorder; and understanding more clearly the role of medication in treatment so they would have had less negative feelings toward it. As parents, we can help give all of these things.

As your child grows, some of the symptoms will begin to dissipate as they are worked on, and some symptoms that may have been mild or less significant may become more severe or prevalent. This is due not only to the way AD/HD manifests itself but also to the fact that this type of change happens with all children. There will always be some situation that calls for your attention.

So when does it all end? Well, you're a parent—you should know that answer. It ends the day you stop caring and being concerned for your child. In other words, it never ends. What I can tell you is that you have a wonderful opportunity as the parent of a child with AD/HD. Be careful—your child just might teach you courage and patience, creativity and curiosity, tolerance and unconditional love. This life is what you make of it, and so, to a great degree, is your child.

Appendix

AD/HD Diagnostic Criteria

$\mathcal{P}$rofessionals who diagnose AD/HD use the diagnostic criteria established in 1994 by the American Psychiatric Association, as listed in the fourth edition of the *Diagnostic and Statistical Manual of Mental Disorders* (DSM-IV). The DSM-IV categorizes the symptoms into three subtypes of the disorder:

- Combined type: Multiple symptoms of inattention, impulsivity, and hyperactivity

- Predominantly inattentive type: Multiple symptoms of inattention with few, if any, symptoms of hyperactivity-impulsivity

- Predominantly hyperactive-impulsive type: Multiple symptoms of hyperactivity-impulsivity with few, if any, symptoms of inattention

Six or more of the nine characteristics in each of the following two groupings must be endorsed for a diagnosis of AD/HD. If six or more characteristics are identified from the inattention grouping, then a diagnosis of AD/HD, predominantly inattentive type, is possible. If six or more characteristics are found for the hyperactivity-impulsivity grouping, then a diagnosis of AD/HD, predominantly hyperactive-impulsive type, is possible. If six or more characteristics from both groupings occur, then a diagnosis of AD/HD, combined type, is possible.

Symptoms of Inattention

1. Often fails to give close attention to details or makes careless mistakes in schoolwork, work, or other activities.

2. Often has difficulty sustaining attention in tasks or play activities.

3. Often does not seem to listen when spoken to directly.

4. Often does not follow through on instructions and fails to finish schoolwork, chores, or duties in the workplace (not due to oppositional behavior or failure to understand instructions).

5. Often has difficulty organizing tasks and activities.

6. Often avoids, dislikes, or is reluctant to engage in tasks that require sustained mental effort (such as schoolwork or homework).

7. Often loses things necessary for tasks or activities (i.e., toys, school assignments, pencils, books, or tools).

8. Is easily distracted by extraneous stimuli.

9. Is often forgetful in daily activities.

Symptoms of Hyperactivity-Impulsivity

Hyperactivity

1. Often fidgets with hands or feet or squirms in seat.

2. Often leaves seat in classroom or in other situations in which remaining seated is expected.

3. Often runs about or climbs excessively in situations in which it is inappropriate (in adolescents or adults, may be limited to subjective feelings of restlessness).

4. Often has difficulty playing or engaging in leisure activities quietly.

5. Is often "on the go" or often acts as if "driven by a motor."

6. Often talks excessively.

Impulsivity

7. Often blurts out answers before questions have been completed.

8. Often has difficulty awaiting turn.

9. Often interrupts or intrudes on others (for example, butts into conversations or games).

Bibliography and References

Alexander-Roberts, C. (1994). *The ADHD parenting handbook.* Dallas: Taylor.

American Psychiatric Association. (1994). *Diagnostic and statistical manual of mental disorders* (4th ed.). Washington, DC: Author.

Barkley, R. (1990). *Attention Deficit Hyperactivity Disorder: Handbook for diagnosis and treatment.* New York: Guilford.

Barkley, R. (1995). *Taking charge of AD/HD.* New York: Guilford.

Crary, E. (1990). *Pick up your socks.* Seattle, WA: Parenting Press.

Dobson, J. (1978). *The strong-willed child.* Wheaton, IL: Tyndale.

Dreikurs, R. (1990). *Children: The challenge.* New York: Penguin.

Elkind, D. (1981). *The hurried child.* Reading, MA: Addison Wesley.

Fisher, G., & Cummings, R. (1990). *The survival guide for kids with LD.* Minneapolis: Free Spirit.

Galvin, M., & Ferrano, S. *Otto learns about his medicine.* New York: Magination.

Garber, S.M., Garber, M., & Freedman-Spizman, R. (1995). *Is your child hyperactive?* New York: Villard.

Hallowell, E.M., & Ratey, J.J. (1996). *Driven to distraction.* New York: Bantam.

Ingersoll, B. (1988). *Your hyperactive child: A parent's guide to coping with Attention Deficit Disorder.* New York: Doubleday.

Kurcinka, M. (1991). *Raising your spirited child.* New York: Harper Collins.

Kvols, J. (1993). *Redirecting children's behavior.* Gainesville, FL: INCAF Publications.

Latham, P.S., & Latham, P.H. (1992). *Attention Deficit Disorder and the law: A guide for advocates.* Washington, DC: JKL Communications.

McCullough, B., & Walker, S. (1981). *401 ways to get your kids to work at home.* New York: St. Martins.

Montessori, M. (1964). *The Montessori method.* New York: Schocken Books.

Moss, D. (1989). *Shelley, the hyperactive turtle.* Rockville, MD: Woodbine House.

Parker, H. (1992). *The ADD hyperactivity handbook for schools.* San Luis Obispo, CA: Impact.

Quinn, P., & Stern, J. (1991). *Putting on the brakes.* New York: Magination.

Taylor, J. (1994). *Helping your hyperactive/attention deficit child.* Rockland, CA: Prima.

Turecki, S. (1989). *The difficult child.* New York: Bantam.

U.S. Department of Education, Office of Special Education and Rehabilitative Services. (1991). *Clarification of policy to address the needs of children with Attention Deficit Disorders within general and/or special education* (Memorandum to Chief State School Officers). Washington, DC: Author.

Weiss, L. (1992). *Attention Deficit Disorder in adults.* Dallas: Taylor.

Wender, P. (1987). *The hyperactive child, parent, and adult.* New York: Oxford University Press.

For access to more information about AD/HD and the locations of local support groups, contact the national offices of Children and Adults with Attention Deficit Disorders (ChADD). Write ChADD, 499 N.W. 70th Avenue, Suite 101, Plantation, FL 33317, or telephone 954–587–3700.

For subscription information about the newsletter *Putting on the Brakes: An Interactive Newsletter for Kids with ADHD,* write Magination Press, a division of Brunner/Mazel, Inc., 19 Union Square West, New York, NY 10003, or telephone 1–800–825–3089 (212–924–3344 in New York).

Index

About the Author

$\mathcal{J}$anet Morris is a certified teacher, AD/HD parenting consultant, and member of ChADD: Children and Adults with Attention Deficit Disorders. She is the director of the Families of AD/HD Children Empowerment Series (FACES) and teaches the FACES course, conducts workshops, and speaks publicly on issues relating to AD/HD. A certified preprimary teacher, she taught and worked with children of various ages prior to consulting full time. Currently attending the University of Michigan and pursuing a master's degree, she resides in Monroe, Michigan, with her two children, Ashley and Alex.

Alex, Janet, and Ashley, 1998